MERCY OF TIDES

Mercy of Tides

POEMS FOR A BEACH HOUSE

EDITED BY Margot Wizansky

ILLUSTRATIONS BY JP Powel

Salt Marsh Pottery Press

Dartmouth, Massachusetts

2003

Salt Marsh Pottery Press
1167 Russells Mills Road
S. Dartmouth, MA 02748-1015

© 2003 by Margot Wizansky

ISBN 0-9742388-0-5

Printed in the United States
Acknowledgements for the poems included
appear on page 213

In memory of Caroline, my friend who taunted the riptide

CONTENTS

THE SPELL AND THE RAPTURE

ON LOVE AND OTHER MISERIES

INTRODUCTION

Antidote to our suffering the state of the world, a poem can gather us in suspiration, that reflexive sigh of recognition, through slightly parted lips. I believe everyone, inlander or not, has a relationship with the place where earth turns to water, and that all of us will find solace in a book of poems set in that place. And so I placed an ad for poems for a beach anthology.

Poems, giant envelopes of poems from thirty-one states and several countries, plunged into my foyer like dolphins. Some poets sent dozens, photocopied from their books. One piece was written by a group of students from Marlboro College traveling in Cuba. I was moved by the openness and generosity with which all of the writers, the well-published and the unpublished, offered their work.

I had asked for fresh images and got them:

> *and I am tempted*
> *to curl in his cool curve,*
> *foamy with pearls*
> > (Mary Ann Larkin.)

> *I come here to lose my mind*
> > (Grace Bauer.)

> *…its chaste astonishing skin smooth as a headstone*
> > (the late Rad Smith.)

Nostalgia:
> *sound of summer when summer wasn't time*
> *but place*
> > (Barbara Helfgott Hyett)

Regret:

> *And the man*
> *she waits for isn't me*
>> (David Starkey)

Loneliness:

> *where your naked feet do not run wet*
> *through the rooms*
>> (Martin Levine)

Grief:

> *You can't make love to a ghost*
>> (Allen West)

Balm:

> *...when we reopened*
> *each other's wounds,*
> *water closed behind us...*
>> (Michael Foster)

Love:

> *...what is between us,*
> *is no matter of choice, but more like*
> *these tides...*
>> (Raphael Kosek)

A few of the poems I solicited particularly because they have sounded in my heart for years – Jane Hirschfield's "If the Rise of the Fish", Carol Dine's "At Sea", and Mark Doty's "Long Point Light":

> *here is nine o'clock, harbor-wide,*
> *and a glinting code: promise and warning.*
> *The morning's the size of heaven.*
>
> *What will you do with it?*

At a beach house, in the outdoor shower, I was surprised by a praying mantis. It stood in the geranium, formal in its morning-coat, swiveled its head and fixed me in its green gaze, so intimate I had to turn away. I need poems to unveil what is baffling, mesmerizing, a confrontation with an insect, the specks that inhabit a tide pool, the carcass of a whale.

So complicated, our connection with the sea, backdrop for our personal dramas, screen on which we project our longings, our most profound fear. The sea gushes its waste and spill; we sift through its leavings for treasure. On certain days it casts a spell on us, days when the shimmer of noon dissolves the horizon and we stay too long in the sun. Some of us find comfort in the cold bite of it, off-season. Some want noisy crowds of other bathers.

Before the sea we are small and helpless; we do our penance, ask for absolution. For all that is dark and unknowable, the sea is astounding, like poetry.

Margot Wizansky
March, 2003

Hermit Crab
Golfito, 03.31.01

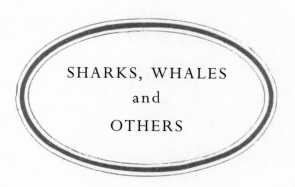

SHARKS, WHALES
and
OTHERS

ROBERT PINSKY

The Want Bone

The tongue of the waves tolled in the earth's bell.
Blue rippled and soaked in the fire of blue.
The dried mouthbones of a shark in the hot swale
Gaped on nothing but sand on either side.

The bone tasted of nothing and smelled of nothing,
A scalded toothless harp, uncrushed, unstrung.
The joined arcs made the shape of birth and craving
And the welded-open shape kept mouthing O.

Ossified cords held the corners together
In groined spirals pleated like a summer dress.
But where was the limber grin, the gash of pleasure?
Infinitesimal mouths bore it away,

The beach scrubbed and etched and pickled it clean.
But O I love you it sings, my little my country
My food my parent my child I want you my own
My flower my fin my life my lightness my O.

RAD SMITH

Requiem Shark

for Rena

This morning as I gulp five gleaming white
capsules of shark cartilage
to make me strong again, I want
another look at the terrible
eye with its nictitating membrane,
those extravagant fins,
the ampullae of Lorenzini freckling its snout,
all of that huge body on the rippled sand
in turtle grass
with an entourage of neon-blue barjacks,
and a remora wriggling in
and out of its gill-slits.
I even want to touch it again,
and this time not just with my fingertips,
but my palm, loveline and lifeline,
my wrist, the underside of my forearm.
I want to press my cheek against its chaste
astonishing skin smooth as a headstone,
want the touch that feels like a blow,
the summoning touch, the touch
of reckoning, the consummating touch, as well as
the stinging sand blown touch of regret,
the stranger's touch on the train,
the reproachful touch,
even the last touch of a human
who has lain down with a shark,
the touch I have spent my life so ignorant of,
your touch as you unbutton my shirt,
the searing, unbearable touch.

KAREN SCOON

The Humpback Whale on Vincent Beach

One couldn't say exactly where
the sluggish swimming stopped
and the parasites finally took over.
What is left of her billows and shreds
in the waves. How she got here like this
with the tide digging trenches around her—
who could know? Come closer and what is
half-sunk might heal you. Whalers used to
crawl inside and let the oil drip down anointing
battered joints and other places in their body lacking vigor.

SUSAN BAZETT

A Photograph Dying of Whales

after a photograph by Monika Andersson

The tide stalled in its wet retreat.
A few figures held at a distance,
who must realize the upturned boats
are whales.
What kindness brought them here?
We cannot save them; they belong
to the water they wish they had not left.
The next day begins to plan itself.
The sea takes and takes. Grey dulls.
Gulls please their tongues.
Nothing is lost. In time we will take home
sea-cleaned bones. The photographer
had trouble walking upon that sand
who took the first light
of remembered day.

MATTHEW S. SISSON

Please, Call Me Moby

I admit he has a certain amount of charisma
and I'm sorry about the leg, it was self defense.
I've had plenty of bad moments over this thing too.
I keep asking myself: Why Me?

I've always minded my own business. God knows
why he's still stalking me. I don't hold anyone's personal
limitations against them, but it's clear the guy has problems.

I've got a heart as big as an eat-in kitchen, but I've had enough
of his bad mouthing. He's publicly cursed my name and accused me
of being malicious. Who started this whole thing?

For crying out loud, he was the one who attacked me.
I'm not a vigilante, but I don't know how much more of this
I can take. It's like the guy just can't take *no* for an answer.

JACQUELINE KUDLER

Bahia de Ballenas

Slap of grey water at the side
of the hull, sea smells, gasoline,
the outboard idling down
to a soft staccato.
Tail! Tail! he cries, swinging
the tiller across his knees
At one o'clock, senora!
The great grey fan opens before us,
balances a moment, plunges below.
Grey skies part for a single shaft
of sunlight.
Twice more she comes, Senora!
Mira! Mira!
Top of the water turns slick.
Broad back glistening in a fine
frost of barnacles, she floats
alongside the way the dark shape of
a dream can float alongside you
all morning long, then disappear.
But first she breathes
(ten suns shimmer in the ripples of her fins)
and we alongside her breathe,
sharing the pleasure of air.

PAMELA USCHUK

Counting Humpback Whales Off Cape Cod

Flippered sister, you shush to the surface, break
iced water with your dense spine.
From spent air, you sigh a fountain
that shatters sky into rainbows.
I've looked for you everywhere—the Pacific,
the Caribbean, Mediterranean,
Aegean, Ionic, the warm Sea of Cortez—
and now you and your sisters gather like a tribe
of tourists to watch this research vessel
toss on the North Atlantic's frigid black flesh.
My earliest memories are of being a panther lying
in the wide eye of sun, juniper scenting my tongue,
the thick pulse of milk in my many breasts,
the tug of my heartblood
at the step of a doe rattling leaves
or of being a wolf, howling at the haunches of my childhood
through blue drifts of midnight tundra, snow
cracking the leather moons of my paws.
Still, in my dreams, lizards
and rabbits, coyotes and eagles talk to me, but you
humpback queen of dark water, you sing
through every cell of my longing,
through unquenchable emptiness
that never stops hoping for love.
For love. You echo my heart, my blood
so that I can barely stand to watch you breech
like an elegant tongue a hundred yards and millennium away.
I have all I can do not to leap
after you, to lay along the mammalian caress of your side
before the end of this century takes us totally out of the world.

JOHN GREY

A Whale of a Story

Let me take a boat
out of the harbor,
into the plankton banks.
Let me cut the engine,
drift atop the gentle swell,
ruddered by the silence.
Let me hug the rail
as the whale soars
out of the stillness,
his massive black back
pitching and rolling,
his tail swooping up and down
like giant gull wings.
Let us hang together
in mid-air
like held breath.
Let me feel the exultant spray
of his plunge
beneath the surface
all over my awe-struck face.
Let me cruise back to land,
nerves tingling,
heart pumping,
as if I've been the sole witness
to the major event
of the century.
Let me read the newspaper
next morning
and see none of this mentioned.

VIV WOODHEAD

Octopus, Tortola

I reach for the conch—
my wrist, bound at once
by whipcord that grips.
I pull away,
electrified.
Intelligence scrolls down
its tentacle, as, camouflaged,
it observes the world through its skin,
indistinguishable
from its property. It knows
I am strong and curious: it retreats,
blanched, affronted,
gun-turret eye-slits horizontal,
body textured like a scrotum.
I had not thought to feel so much
sympathy with anything inhuman,
out of my element.

STEVEN ABLON

Cod Washed Ashore

More rigid than the bones
of whales, the gills lock open,
glass eyes covered in sand,
wind plucking out the cheeks,
sun bending back the skin.
He trembles. He is dead.
He knows everything,
the way a white pigeon
charms full skirted palms,
and white blossoms
fall from the orange.

ERIC LEIGH

Hammer Point, Florida

A boy sits by the canal and listens to water purl
against the cement walls. They appear suddenly—

only their mouths above the surface and the sound
of their breath—manatees. The boy feeds them lettuce

stolen from the crisper tray, drops leaves that swirl
in the current as the animals inhale and pull them close.

With father's flashlight he can see scars on their backs,
white against gray skin; one is missing half its tail.

He draws them in with spray from the garden hose.
They are next to him in the sound of rain, mouths

opening wide as he waters; they drink leisurely.
Then he lets it go by, this chance to swim with manatees,

to feel scars and barnacle-covered skin, to ask them
how many boys are out on a night like this,

feeding them stolen vegetables and watering the ocean.

MIKHAIL HOROWITZ

Feeding Fiddlers

For maybe an hour at low tide
I watched them from the road, a brackish water
fiddlers' convention, foraging crabs in a slow, turgid, seething
pavane, a stately & faintly disgusting gavotte, the males leading
with those aberrant claws, crafted by some crustacean Stradi-
varius of the baroque Devonian, but the sound they make is
not Scarlatti, it's a scarcely audible, almost ghostly
hissing, the pianissimo of tiny mastication, as
thousands upon thousands crawl the exposed
flats in quest of comestibles, filtering
food alfresco from the black café of
mud, finally retreating (unsated,
one imagines) to minuscule
bungholes in the mire, the
tide coming back & the
dance of appetite
done.

DAVID GIANNINI

from **"To The Wave"**

Gulls
    squabbling on rocks, a tyranny of beaks
cocked in territory/
                jetty …swaggarts'
combustible struts —— desire that tweaks
(availability of shells)
             and remains Desire

'no one not in need'

No one not in need
would think these gulls
sacred —— instead
recognize in calls

something of the ruthless
something of the fierce

"What were we, then,
Before the being of ourselves began?"

—— lost and fierce!
indistinct
but that instinct:

Desire that remains Desire
No one not in need.

SUELLEN WEDMORE

Gulls in June

A gull chick tumbles from the wild
roses, a black-back dives; I thrust a stick
above my head to hold back the murderous

nurturing—it's the nestlings' squeals that prick
gulls to this frenzy: the scouring
of the shore for clams, moon snails;

shells flung onto granite ledge,
laying open plush bellies.
Once I too was bound to the tides

of a newborn's hunger, cries
that blurred day's rise and fall,
breasts engorged with the fierceness

of suckling. A black-back
with its chick nearby
stabs a herring gull

with the pincers of its beak;
blood curdles. Wings spasm.
What is love? What

survival? I hurl a stone
at the seagull's frenzied cry.

PAUL HAMILL

Treading

Still the gatherers come, moving
In the glare as if dazed,
Treading, stooping.

I hunt beyond them, neck-deep
At the channel's slope,
Turning
In a lazy whale's ballet.

I drift to the edge of shock,
Plunging
To grasp

Bulging cockles, nubbed
Conches, black-ridged clams.
When I have hauled them home

I eat them raw, their pink
Tough sweetness drenched in lemon
Or vodka; and then I sleep,
Sliding down channels of dream.

SHELBY ALLEN

Conch

Wrapped in its own story,
this life whorled a castle
-- rough turrets, pink fluting --
for its core, soft and small.

Alone on the sand, a dropout
from the waves of give and take,
it survives like a showoff,
its flares get fancier every year.

I want this hard beauty.

I take the shell home,
unpack it,
smell death: the pronged stink
of what stays coiled inside.

I run water over and over --
this won't wash through.
The underside of my shell
is a mouth: two lips calcified open,
not for words, just the crying
jumping out of me,
heaving
hard sounds.

WILLIAM GREENWAY

Dancing With Sharks

We've seen them caught, know
they're here, five- and six-footers,
        but we hold each other and dance,
pressing close in the salty dark
        gumbo-thick with plankton and the spray
of a trillion eggs like the stars overhead.
        And when I enter the oyster folds
of her, we feel things sliding
        between our legs, restless
with their slick skins
        and endless appetites.

SIMMONS B. BUNTIN

A Gathering

Assateague's wind-littered beach
meets me, often, on violent mornings:
early spring, the limp crucifix

of tangled skate. Or the hard autumn
freeze on fallow fields. Today
I came across a hermit,

a combination of weathered shell
and invertebrate detail. Courting
the surf's edge, he contemplated

whelk, settled lightly
on battered carapace, and gorged.
As I approached the single

feast—intricate crab workings,
imprecise red claw and eyes—
he disappeared into the undertow. As waves

like shipwrecks then crashed
in the crescendo of the scene,
minimal armies relished in their creel,

black-headed gulls were born
of drifting chicken bones, and I
turned toward my Olds
and felt the wind consume the sea.

JEANNETTE I. WINTHROP

Something to Keep

for my grandchildren

A body of a tern,
how it came to be here,
or how it died, maybe,
in the night's storm, I can't say.
What do I know of birds?

I find no shell,
no stone on the beach,
no treasure
I want to give years from now,
water washed to its perfection.
Look, I could say, *this is what I found*
at the shore before any of you
learned to walk.

Only the tern,
half-buried in sand like some
black, gray rag, head twisted behind,
looks back from where it came.

Glass Bottomed Boat

for Sara

Along the coast, mangroves hug
rusty soil, roots tentative

as the daughter's visits from college,
can't wait to leave,

doesn't know yet that life
has a way of doing its own teaching.

I see a pelican enter the water cleanly,
wings folded like a broken umbrella.

The boat stops. Huge sea turtles
swim below. They glide

in one direction, the boat rocks in the other.
Nausea draws me up and back

to cooler air. By the time the idling motor
starts again, I've arranged and rearranged

all the furniture of my mind, room after room
and still I haven't got it right.

RONALD PIES

St. Maarten's Fire

In a greenblue nest
  of shoal and sea,
tucked away
  from Caribbean gale
and roiling wave,
  we snorkeled past
some fire coral,
  battering
with our flippers
  their millennial home.
With the first
  needle-burn buzz,
we thought
  we'd cut our arms
on crusted rock—
  but the blaze
drawn down our nerves
  was coral's sting;
silent, communal,
  in the end, benign—
the grave signature
  of who rules this place.

JENNIFER LAURA JOHNSON

Pyractomena Borealis

The lightning bugs
were trapped
on the sand
at Ocean Grove.
Fleshy sea foam
arrested their wings.

We tracked them down
guided by
their waning luminescence
their tiny lanterns
flickering
on and off
Help us
we
are
drowning.

I don't know why
they were on the beach that night.
But I loved you then
with your callused hands
cupped
like you knew you were holding
something much bigger
something much more precious.

Captain Tom's
Golfito, Costa Rica 03·27·01 JR.

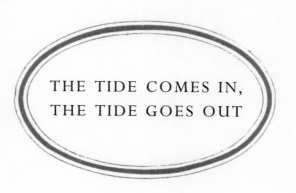

THE TIDE COMES IN,
THE TIDE GOES OUT

WILLIAM PITT ROOT

Ways Water Has

It always moves and pleases me, these ways
the ocean has with walls of adamant—urgent and lavish,
restless as the moon, persistent as darkness;
even the lesser wave as it meets stone
breaks into brilliance
and that fluent whisper riotous in the graceful rush of foam.

And look,
see how these reefs admit and shed what washes over them,
resisting and absorbing, in one stance, the myriad approaches
            of the sea,
and how carelessly the simple water fondles, shocks
and undermines the fundamental granite
touch by touch.

That innocent reduction of the upright cliff
to puffs and swirls of dust
the wingbeat of the least seabird can scatter!

May I know a woman who has known the sea.

PAUL WILLIS

Refugio

The palm-lined beach is hollow in its sweep,
the point break spins the rollers long and slow;
one surfer pulls a headstand on his board,
approaching sand as sky, and sky as sand.

In December 1812 a tidal wave
snapped a Boston ship, *The Mercury*, from anchor
and sent it surging inland up the creek
a full half mile, rushing through the tops
of sycamore, through groves of flooded oak.

Between the hills the water lost its force
and sucked itself backrushing to the sea,
the schooner with it, sliding swift, intact,
the sailors at the rails, amazed with fear,
but certain, if they made it past the shore,
that nothing else in their reverted lives
could ever really take them by surprise.

MARC J. STRAUS

4 PM: The Blue of Mahoe Bay

Turquoise, indigo, azure, cerulean—
      cadmium-blue? Pearly adjectives
are even worse. It's like the painter. She can squeeze
      from fifty different tubes—a little more
rose—something closer to indigo. Some days
      it's just never quite right. Let's say

we had a sea storm yesterday, that in the last
      two hours the sand has sifted out, that the
brain coral reflects back a spill of orange
      and taupe. Let's say the sun is climbing down
the crease between Neckar and Peter's beach, that
      a three-mast schooner angles south of the Dogs,

that the surf wrinkles lightly with a milky lip
      on a velvet blanket of new butternut sand, that
a little girl, maybe three, sits by the edge with those red
      water balloons on her arms, that she sees
a hermit crab, that her blue eyes sparkle—blue,
      blue against the blue sea.

LAURENCE SNYDAL

Straits

When I sidle down the sliding rise
Of sand and smell the salt and hear
The sighing of the sea that lies
And rolls and lies against my ear,
I am an angel. Over these
Grey rocks and this grey water I
Am sentinel. All at my ease
I saunter on the shore and shy
Sand dollars at the sea. I make
My footprints marking out a known
Where no known was. I seize and shake
The tide and tie it to a stone.
I lay my life out on this sand
And salt. I watch the breakers fall,
I hold that breaking in my hand.
The sea makes children of us all.

JAMES DOYLE

Small Seascape

I have my head so close
to a tidal pool in the rocks
I could be fishing with my nose,
trying to replace air with water
as my face's natural limit
and magnifying glass. What I see
are grits with no eyes
and barely enough body, swimming,
darting, cutting right angles
and a sudden hypotenuse
into an element that can't hold
for more than a turn or two
the quart of water the last wave
could spare by a factor
in the millions. If a crab
were my centerpiece in this instant
living room, liquid, porous,
ready to collapse itself
and travel to the next site
at a moment's notice,
like a miniature circus,
I'd be so taken by size
and recognizable shape, I'd miss
the real performers, the fleas,
the specks, incidental networks
of perpetual motion, turning
their tricks like pros
no matter how movable the hoops,
the stages, they are given,

no matter how gargantuan
their competitors, how capricious
the ocean they seem
to have no trouble
reducing to size.

NATASHA SAJÉ

Channel

after Henry Vaughan

Water
      you are, not were nor will be—

          as cataracts & creeks, as river brown as trout,
              as kidney and as skin.

                  Water you *are,* not were

                                      nor will be
              rolling ocean green or
quiet

      without wind enough to twirl the one red leaf.

                  What channel does my soul seek?

This—

      snow melting from trees like rain, a clean rinsing,
         a quickness the sun has kissed—

      and this—salt desert water swollen with birds feasting
             on brine flies feasting on algae—

and this—siphoned through sulfurous rock, glacier
old as amaranth.

I stray and roam.

To be useful, to be clear—

LAURA LECHNER

Landscape

Yesterday's work, the marsh
beyond my shoulder, lies
drying on the ground,
the reeds then
just hummocky, beige.
The weave of the canvas
distinct through thin paint.

Should I stoke the landscape
with a swath of tangerine?
There is orange in the sunlit
puzzle of grasses at low tide
where the dunes recede.

Who can know how beauty grows?
How quickly the tide
will reappear, obscuring
what I have failed to see?
The grass twists and bends
under the wind's benediction,
glints of yellow in the blades.

CAROLINE KNOX

Pantoum du chat

Charles and I go out together
in his boat, which is a cat-
amaran, in the burnishing weather,
elated, so it's not surprising that

in his boat, which is a cat
at top speed among cats, this poem begins.
Elated, so it's not surprising that
we sing "Speed Bonnie Boat" to the winds.

At top speed among cats, this poem begins
making me seasick. "This malady," says Charles, "will become,
as we sing 'Speed Bonnie Boat' to the winds,
as naught," preventing them from

making me seasick. "This malady," says Charles, "will become
the narrative wave of the future, the wave of metaphor,
the wave of Narragansett Bay, of foam.
All the cliché for cats: liquid, longueur, languor,

the narrative wave. Of the future: the wave of metaphor,
I say, will be transfigured by the cat.
All the cliché for cats: liquid, longueur, languor,
as among poems this wave begins that

I say will be transfigured by the cat
as the cat leaps, you know, in timely weather."
All this of course in a Catamaran Voice, the times that
Charles and I go out together.

DONNA HILBERT

Peninsula

Finger connected to the hand
by an isthmus of land.

I live on one,
travel to another to recover.

Yuke-a-tawn, Jack says, correcting my pronunciation.

At home, the bay on one side,
ocean on the other.

Here, it's ocean and sea.

Peninsula. Might as well be an island
where I've washed up
salty, alone.

ZACK ROGOW

At Gualala Beach

      tough wind
             throws my voice
   back down my throat

      waves mutter
as they shake themselves out
            against all that is stationary
   their edges
    heavy cream

           wild yellow
      poppies
 flutter on brittle
       orange
       cliffs

         redwood driftwood
smoothed and twisted
    knee joint
       of imaginary beast
   worm-eaten
in reverse Braille
         half-rune half
      Japanese calligraphy
  what does it spell

BARBARA HELFGOTT HYETT

Vacation

1.

At the bay, the minnows
seem to kiss me, take
my legs into their mouths.
I can't count their see-through
bodies, blue-spotted foreheads,
as if they had foreheads. Spawned
into this instant, those tiny fish
are feeding. They are ravenous.
I am all they have.

2.

You don't worship me, he says,
eyes on the marsh, arms stretched
on the table before him. *I love you,*
I answer behind him, my palm brushing
his hair. *I want to be adored,* he says.
I kiss the top of his head lightly.
I love you, and now I am stroking
his shoulder. This very shoulder. This hair.
It is late afternoon. The beach still clings
to my thighs. I am smiling. The tide in
its fragrance continues to turn.

3.

In the shower, I turn my back
to the tiles, refuse the soap, let
my hair take the water in and hold
it there . . . I think of his toes,

their perfect roundness. I think of the power
in his hands. All of my life is water,
and whatever I fear is water also.

The Inlet

Here again, the rough-cut jetty, the ridge
worn flat by men trolling bass and bluefish
and boys with plastic buckets full of porgies.
The hooks are taut in their mouths.
I comb the crevices for mussels, find
a baby flounder, stiff and gray, a shell.
Right side down a huge crab bakes on a rock.

Behind me, vacant, boarded up, the tenements.
Where I was born. Beige bricks, three or four stories
crammed with families, fathers who delivered milk
or sold potato chips from tall tin cans—
I scooped them into brown bags, watched the oil seep through.

In summers, mothers gave up unemployment
to work in the tourist places hawking beach chairs,
vegematics, tickets to *Ripley's Believe It or Not*.
Mothers didn't swim. They sent us to stay
at the lifeguard stand with a quarter for lunch.
We'd swim past the jetty to the rotted pilings, then back
to the shallows and the puckered seaweed. I'd open my eyes
underwater, watch the silversides skimming my cheek.
When my towel underneath the boardwalk was all in shadow
and the sand had turned quartz cold, I went home.

At Zwiebacks, after dinner, I'd read comic books
or else I'd buy one used. Later, at Altman Field
the boys from Philly who stayed at the guest house
would start to shoot some baskets.
Sometimes I'd just sit on the bleachers
licking salt from the back of my hand.
Everything was like that then: crisp, expectable,
a silent movie, the ocean and the hoop disappearing
gradually from the end of the playground
until I couldn't see the ball anymore.

In my bed, I'd watch the sway of the clotheslines
on the rooftop outside my window and listen
to the men playing pinochle at the dining-room table,
the stogie smoke gray and small-winged down the hall.
The women swept the floors, laid roach traps,
ate chocolate at the mahjongg game downstairs.
They'd laugh, and clack the bone-faced tiles,
a sound of summer when summer wasn't time
but place, ordinary as the low cry of a loon
diving at night, the voice of a beach block,
its muggy rhythm, the click of the tide
just before it turns.

RAPHAEL KOSEK

Seascape 3

The blue purple china of scavenged mussel shells
tumbles over and over helplessly with each wave.

The seagulls are here with me looking
for whatever may turn up. They will take

whatever comes their way
and so will I: a lustrous bit of shell

or a moonstone that catches my eye.
The water mesmerizes, claiming the sand

beneath my feet, reminding me how easily
it all shifts about until everything is different

and we can't recognize where we've been.
But the wash and gurgle, the watery hiss

of each new round, presses thoughts of you
upon me, one after another, pushing me

into belief that what is between us,
is no matter of choice, but more like

these tides that roam the earth from continent
to continent, listing toward a pale gold moon.

AMY DENGLER

Watering the Lavender at Sunset

This could be Provence:
lush purple spilling over the front steps
bees stunned by the fragrance
a seabreeze stirring the black-eyed Susans.

The harbor this afternoon was bobbing with vessels.
We bought fish and fixed supper in the yard,
the tablecloth luffing up
before we moored it with silver and plates.
When the sky opened we stayed put, watched
the haddock swim again on the platter
the wineglasses fill with rain
the candles sputter out.

Lavender anchors me here,
so too a freshening breeze,
slack lines singing in the boatyards.
Tomorrow, all the ceremonies will be the same:
first light, cast off, mug-up,
saltwater lapping enameled hulls, seamusic
essential as air.

When Audrey Hepburn Returns

She comes at dusk—
a white bird
autographing the evening with elegance.
On lanky legs and yellow feet
she settles into the marsh
and surveys the creek, her neck
momentarily forgetting its curve.
She folds in her silk sleeves.

At first light when the marsh is all chatter and splash,
she will reinvent flight.
What we will remember is a hush of wings
like the rustle of taffeta,
and the marsh
forming and reforming,
flooding the deep and the shallows.

WILLIAM JOHN WATKINS

Brothers & Fish

brothers and fish, my sons
spread their hair on the water, five and six
under the laughing waves and over
tumble the summer days

father and dolphin, my beard spreads
on the water twenty and eight
under the graying waves and over
edge the summer days

MARY ANN COLEMAN

Escaping the Sea

Tidewaters of the Atlantic
skim twilight to shore.
Waves lapse to the sea's hollow.
Snail shells, oysters, jingles
flow toward us, spin and are gone.
Sandpiper's prints, tracks of fiddler crab.

Clouds shift on the intricate sand.

Floating in your arms
which rock like rented boats
I want to live forever, think
of the dorsal fins of sharks
lifting out of rough water.

Come, I'll give you
a conch shell for our aging house,
a ghost sound of the sea.

Playa del Este, Cuba

Cuba, 2001

Yemaya rests where the waters of Oshun meet the waters of the sea.
Waves lap at her feet and trickle down to the sand.
I twist my hair and lift it off the nape of my neck—looking out.
In 1994 many Cubans left from this beach
in small fishing boats and inner tubes. Today in the overcast
of late rainy season, I wonder what were their prayers?
I would pray to Yemaya every day of my life
to live on a beach as beautiful as Santa Maria,
O Barra Su Ayo!
Water purifies, air sustains; everywhere
in the tropics water meets the land and coral, shells
are crushed into sand where palm trees grow.
Sweet slumber was my day;
thoughts of la playa played in my mind;
happy was I . . .
later I still felt the tides moving my blood.

JOHN WYLAM

December 31, 3 a.m., Daytona Beach

That wall of lights, curving slightly west,
then back toward the Atlantic, a lighthouse
at the pier marking this town's last surviving
revelers, most of them local, bikers
and beachcombers long out of luck,
all of them drunk by now, waiting
at the wooden railing as low tide teases them
a little further out. The bars' neon signs
go dark; Atlantic Avenue
awaits tomorrow night's comedy, the year's
turning again.

The hotels are half-empty; the town, in fact,
somnolent and slow, never quite sleeps.
Not even the tide cares anymore,
exposing fish for seagulls milling about on the beach,
their dull hunger still saying nothing
about this other life, at the shadow-side of Paradise.
You won't find it at the lighthouse,
though the locals could lead you to it
from there, if they wanted. Better to walk south
along the beach, past the barricades and cold hotels
where tourists sleep off their common overdose,
the sun's pitiless and constant enterprise.
Somewhere between Daytona and New Smyrna,
past the wreckage of a wooden boat,
a subtle, small lie,
past the unpainted bungalows, grim
as survivors deserve to be;

keep walking until the hotels' pale-fingered light
gives up on you at last, no matter how long it takes,
and drink the salt straight from the air,
taste it for yourself, tonight, tomorrow, the same.

WENDY DREXLER

Summer Night

At the dance club high above the swell
    of dune, our bodies sway and surge
        in the hot lunge of twelve-bar blues.

The singer in the short red dress dangles
    her high-heeled shoe. She hammers and slides
        the keys, licks the air with love and leaving—

that yellow-throated fire. Later we float down
    to the beach. In moonlight, ocean spills a liquid spine.
        Venus smolders among shimmering prongs of stars.

Waves break and break. We listen
    to grains of sand turn in their pale beds—
        hunger we didn't know we had.

LEE RUDOLPH

The Return

We went to the beach and the beach followed us home.
Sand has found its way into the sugar bowl
water runs salt from the tap
and all night long waves open the doors

                                    and slam them shut
like the blood fumbling in the chambers of our hearts.

November Beach

Though banks of dark clouds hid the sun,
it was being pointed at, not subtly,
by the whole sky, which might as well have been
a medieval panel with a gold leaf glory
pointing at the blank wood in its center
where some saint's face has flaked away.

No matter that there is no face: if we are clever
we can tell which saint it is—the robes, the flower
at the feet, the instruments of torture
and martyrdom, the mascot (lion, dog, bird) . . .
any one of these is better than a signature,
if we have learned to read; although the painter
has and had no signature, no name.

God has hidden his face,
to which the whole creation points,
somebody said. I follow my own footprints
back up the beach, to look a second time
at the sea-snails' elegant, idiot scrawl
on the sandy bottom of the tidal pool.

THE SPELL
and the
RAPTURE

JANE HIRSHFIELD

If the Rise of the Fish

If for a moment
the leaves fell upward,
if it seemed a small flock
of brown-orange birds
circled over the trees,
if they circled then scattered each in
its own direction for the lost seed
they had spotted in tall, gold-checkered grass.
If the bloom of flies on the window
in morning sun, if their singing insistence
on grief and desire. If the fish.
If the rise of the fish.
If the blue morning held in the glass of the window,
if my fingers, my palms. If my thighs.
If your hands, if my thighs.
If the seeds, among all the lost gold of the grass.
If your hands on my thighs, if your tongue.
If the leaves. If the singing fell upward. If grief.
For a moment if singing and grief.
If the blue of the body fell upward, out of our hands.
If the morning held it like leaves.

FREDDY FRANKEL

The Perfect Wave

Cape St. Francis, South Africa

Let me wade out to meet it
where the water rises
from itself—
mount it, stand
and grip my surf-board
with my naked soles.

Four feet in height and two miles wide
it rolls in
regular as my young heartbeat—
won't quit, split or section
till it melts
reaching for the dunes.

Let me slide step by step
toward the nose—
squat beneath the curl
ahead of the break until
my calves ache,
and the pith inside me
leaps!

JOHN MORGAN

The Dive-Master's Manifest

Here is your wet-suit, your tank, this is
the weight-belt, your mouthpiece, your mask,
never called goggles. These are your fins,
not flippers, please, and this is the pressure gauge.

Lean back, let the tank pull you over:
a backwards flip is best for one of your age
and when you bob to the surface, point
to your head like this, making the sign for OK.

The rest is gesture. No sounds but the burble
of exhale, the sonorous inrush of breath.
You must never forget to breathe or the pressure
will shrivel your lungs to the size of a mango seed.

Quickly, as we descend through clouds
of insignificant species—the blues ones that dart
like bees, the gray ones with loud yellow bars,
the angel fish like plates—if your ears feel the weight

of water like heaven's thunder pressing in,
just hold your nose and blow,
as you would on a plane coming down.
A crab is a five-fingered crawl.

When I pinch with thumb and forefinger, making
this sign, observe the barracuda as it lolls
between ridges of coral like an overturned hull
covered with barnacles, covered with lime.

Brain coral's a frothy confection, its surface
of folds like gray matter on which the parrot
fish dine. Should my hands stand erect
as in prayer, beware the shark's silhouette

and mark how thought can shrink
at the sudden appearance of implacable design.
Note the delicate coral fans.
The swaying of fronds from the waves'

deflection at depths resembles a dance
that may recall how small ships in a gale
rock to the beat of the devil's quadrille
till your stomach heaves and throbs—

another adjustment you must make to the deep,
as at evening going to sleep, your bed
has the softness of coral, and shells fill the blanks
of your eye-holes, the sighs of your breathing

forgotten—till a gasp, and you come to yourself
in the ever-remembering water.

DEE LEROY

Broadkill Beach

August

We lie on the altar
of the sun

near remains
of those the ocean chose
to sacrifice this day—

flattened medusa
on the sand,

Limulus
already decayed—

wary
of this star of ours,
the more so for knowing

half its life is past
and tempers flare
in middle age.

It will die rudely,
we are told,

boiling first
the unsuspecting sea,

devouring its planets
in mortal rage.

Already it presses
its small demands:

granting sight, destroying it
if the eye stares back
too hard,

warming us
until we burn.

SONYA TAAFFE

The Drowned Men's Waltz

This is the waltz that the drowned men dance
in the green salt currents of the sea.
This is the dance done with water-locked lungs
where the light is falling through jade.
When the tides take them they jerk and whirl
downward, spiraling, where the light drops away,
where the weeds stream upward, where the cold can crush—
This is the song that the sirens sing
when the sailors dance to their tunes.

KATHRYN KRUGER

Querida

Then she gave him a well-finished adze, and led the way onward
to the far end of the island where there were trees, tall grown,
alder and poplar and pine that towered to the heaven . . .
                              —The Odyssey *(V:237—239)*
                              trans. Richmond Lattimore

Have you outgrown
your island?
Are you eager
to cross the sea?

Prepared to cut timber
and bind it with rope
woven from your will's
strong fibers?

Are you ready to sail
toward a larger purpose
driven by thirst
to the pearl of that shore?

O pilgrim, ravished
by the journey
resolve to set foot
on the soil tilled

by the white flower
of your longing.
Prepare, querida,
to blossom.

The Beachcomber's Art

Once after a storm on Okracoke Island
the menfolk walked the beach.
Sun dazzled the water,
sand reflected the sea's glitter.
They watched tiny crabs tunnel in sand,
watched pipers dance with waves.
They brought back shells and fragments of shells
in fantastic shapes, each with its own story
that began "in a faraway place called home."

They brought back shells and mermaid's purse
and the bones of a whale, yes, the bones of a whale
picked from the skeleton gleaming clean
from tides and storm, the gulls and sun,
rib bones, lithe and curved as flutes should be.
I wish I had gone with them, I would know
what to make of it, now, I would get it right,
cord and whale's rib, some feathers and shells,
maybe then when we hung the amulet
the wind would sing in the bones.

ANNE C. FOWLER

Under the Bridge at Abel's Neck

in the shallows
baby white jellyfish, some smaller
than my thumbnail, undulate over
the rocks, transparent mushroom
caps, untethered parachutes
opening, rhythmically, closing
moving sideways, upside down,
oblivious to the jittering
of crab below, passage
of crayfish.

We wonder how it will be
when eating and breathing and swimming
are all one
when surface and depth
are all one.

The river of God is full of water.

JOANNA CATHERINE SCOTT

The Age of Reason

Flies at the windows,
blood in tiny glasses ...

After church on summer Sundays,
you could fling your Bible
and your sunhat on the bed,
tramp, head on fire, back blistering,
in scrub behind the beach house,
wonder about God.

And drinking blood.
And everlasting flame.

You could run
through spinifex and saltbush,
scratch your legs until the blood ran,
scramble to the hot crest of a sandhill,
fling out your arms,
spreadeagled
on the image of salvation.

You could shout, "Receive my spirit!"
crumple onto sand,
and watch a fly as big as your thumb
come creeping up your leg,
unroll his little trunk

and set the flat black end
against your blood.

GRACE BAUER

Far Out. In Deep.

They turn their backs on the land.
They look at the sea all day.
—Robert Frost

I come here to lose my mind.
That too-inside-myself
part of myself I live in

too much of the time.
Coming back, like so many,
year after year, and again

coming back like the waves
to this beach we come back
to sit on and stare at,

earth and ocean offering
a ritual of return,
a spectacular promise

that recurrence does amount
to something, even if we don't
know what it is. And in the midst

of the expected we find surprise
enough to keep us looking:
the school of dolphins

trawling all afternoon for bluefish;
the sea turtle, a century old
or more, washed up like litter

in the surf; the rainbow that hangs
in the sky above a sailboat
emblazoned with a rainbow:

all this on this ordinary day
at this shore where we come
to waste and gain time, watching

whatever we happen to see
in the sea that keeps lapping
at our lazy feet until

one afternoon—like this one—
we take the plunge—first
wading into the shallows

and then summoned by a wave,
swimming further out and then
out even farther, until we are

almost overwhelmed with being
out of our own element and
submerged in the longing

we have watched for so long
that returning to dry land
feels more like a leaving.

RUTH MOON KEMPHER

The Rivers That Feed the Sea

are a ways from here, only guessed at
in the tides, and what births the salt waters

and what moves the planets
only a guess

but soon it will be moonrise, whether or not we watch
even if we go to town, it will rise

out of our ocean yard, orange
fading to old gold in dilution, and in the process

putting poems to silence.

A finger can trace the rivers' courses
down any map; this is where they rise and this

where they pass through town banks, past houses
factories, gas stations. Here's where they divide

and falter, near where we'd go, maybe one day
down the salt dunes to the sea

following our blood.

And when we've been to town, and seen
the world and its houses, prim and neat—

seen the quiet streets, waiting
for something that might someday happen, then

we can come again, to find
the risen moon, silvering our cupboards.

HALVARD JOHNSON

Seascape

We are surrounded
by the sea, the sea
is all around us.
We are ourselves
in circles of the sea,
ourselves to the end
of the curving sun and sea.
Today is a windy day,
we are so happy.
We are ourselves in
the circles, ourselves
to the ends of the sea.
No wind today,
and we are happy.
We are ourselves in
the sand, the circling sun,
the curling sea, the curving
ends of what we barely see.

REBECCA BAGGETT

Thalassa

It is one of the words that haunt me still:
the alphas like small fish slipping before
and behind the slow break of the sigmas,
the theta solid as the shore at the word's head,
and the lambda protruding from the center
like the white crest of a wave, caught in the moment
before it breaks and remembered like that always.
The soft hiss of the word, with the lisp that begins it,
like the slow constant murmur underlying the waves' roar:
thalassa, thalassa. Or it might be a sound half-heard
in sleep, a poem whispered to you in dreams, forgotten
while waking, or the certainty that though you sail
all the seas of earth, spend your life staring
into unknown waters, not one of them, not one,
will be the sea of which you have dreamed.

ELIZABETH CROWELL

I Know I Should Be Thinking of Poetry

but this morning's clouds clean the blue
and a mile from here the ocean leans
its same slick wave where yesterday
I went with my lover in the dusk
to see a yellow blotch of light
become a single line, underneath the clouds,
refracting on the sea.
I should be paying attention to poetry
but instead the laundry lines' empty clips
repeat for me in rows, gray wood,
like the houses on these streets,
and a single blue sheet goes slack then tight,
steady as a beat.
I should be paying attention to poetry
not the white light on the gravel patio,
the way the chairs invite their slanted circle,
but I sit in one of them and smell
the salt air and paint and roses
and watch a woman hold her brush up
as if she's trying to draw in the air
the strange pause of being unsure
her line will work.
I know I should be paying attention to poetry
but there's the oceanless sound
a seaside-town makes, the steady rumble of trucks
carrying the fish in ice back out
and then there are the heavy names of inns
with words like *Stone, Light, Reach, Home, End,*
and *Moor,* words that ought to be in poems.

RASMA HAIDRI

The Face of Ocean

We are deep mystery.
We are known to no one.

We contain a multitude
of contradictions

woven into one
as the ocean is one

and the sea anemone
and the blue whale within it

are of equal grandeur
and equal insignificance.

CAROL WADE LUNDBERG

Hilo-by-the-Sea

All night long
huge orange and silver carp
sing to each other
in the pond
below our window

their bubbling voices
rising like air
through stone and wood
into the chambers
of my ears as if

I have been carried
beneath the sea
by some unknown desire.
All night long

I heard them calling
through my dreams
while in the harbor
boats rocking
on its silky surface

answer "We are here;
Yes, we too; We
are here; Yes, we too,"

their watery voices
lapping me out
to sea, opening gills
of memory as if

they are singing
to me, as if
through the night
while I thought I slept
I have been calling,
calling, and they have
been answering.

JUDITH STRASSER

Island Eyes

I know the merganser
more by its low, quick quack
than its crest; I need dark glasses
to locate the ore boats
against the winking glare of the lake;
my bifocals smooth the cobbles
to a flat and blurry beach.

It takes several days
to acquire island eyes—

slowing down enough
to see the trace
of an abandoned school house path;
learning that islands
come into focus
when the day is gray and flat;
finding patience to wait for dark
and the blink
of the Raspberry Island light.

WILLIAM HOUSTON

She Sells Seashells

Born and raised poor is likely to have one of two results:
Life long thrift or life long spend-thrift.

I fit usually into the first group which is why I have never
        cruised across the Atlantic or Pacific, stayed in New York or
        San Francisco without crashing with friends, never lived
        in a skyscraper or by the sea although I stayed one night
        in a beach shack before Malibu got hot on the market.

Actually, I've never seriously wished for a house on the ocean
        because the windows always need cleaning and I'd never
        get used to live-in help unless they looked good
        barefoot and better than I do in underwear.

Which isn't just thrift but lack of wherewithal, not believing in
        capitalism because it seldom is benign like monarchs aren't either.
I was raised to believe that a capitalist is as likely to get into
        Heaven as a camel is to crawl through the head of a needle
        which in my case wasn't Dad's sour grapes but a questionable
        principle that has been successful in keeping me from getting rich.

Not that I don't fling it around now and then.
I was going strong for cashews for quite a while, even macadamias, before
        I finally found out I preferred peanuts anyway.

Not that I haven't sat on somebody rich's deck like I lived there, watching
        the ocean, wallowing in philosophical meanders. "Cradle
        endlessly rocking" my foot! The ocean I have seen most often is
        a terror, thrashing itself, ripping at the earth that contains it.

Once in a while it gets regular, quiet, and then "whoosh!" it gets wild again.
    No sweet mother that, more like Ma Whats-her-name who raised
    all her kids to be bank robbers.

Seriously, though, I know what Whitman meant, and if you get far
    enough away and high enough, get the whole picture, not just
    the sea shore, it heaves, rolls, every wave different but like enough
    to get hypnotic and you think about Atlantis, Robinson Crusoe,
    Jacques Cousteau, defying the casual immensity, without clocks, comfortable if
    wary, living with it, whales, seaweed, bones and wrecks on the bottom.

Well, you get the idea. Windows ought to be covered with parts
    of ocean so you don't get too comfortable, too sure of yourself and your
    tiny life.

GLORIA COSGROVE

Our Part of the Earth

In our evening attire
we take our seats
on the beach
preferring to face east
keeping watch
out over the ocean
as the part of the earth
on which we dwell
turns its back
on the sun
and hands over
the stage to the
stars.

LOU MASSON

Cannon Beach, Oregon

morning
Even the wild strawberries
humble themselves before the ocean
grow small and fine
as do most plants in the sandy margin
between the kingdoms of land and sea.

I am no different
as I watch the tide
and in the scrub grass
a black beetle scurrying
unaware of me and the sea.

I stand in the margin of two kingdoms
and look back at my tracks, toes pointing out,
that lie behind me like a herring spine
flushed from the depths to lodge here
between tides with twig, shell, bark, bone.

night
Sleep eludes me as it always does
in the stale neatness of motel rooms.

Our trips to the coast are infrequent,
more so as we grow older.

My thoughts are ritual and migratory,
but you sleep next to me and hold your place.

Perhaps spring, the whales just off the shore,
the geese honking in the darkness overhead

disturb me, make me wonder if migrations
are but place in motion. Does what knows,

what feels, remain stationary despite travel,
despite the wandering of conscience and dream?

I grow tired and your breathing in concert
with the whispering waves laps over me.

I wish to join you, let the sounds lap over me,
sleep, and wake by your side and the sea.

MARJORIE POWER

Beach Tarot

A woman in queen's clothing
tumbles from The Tower,
her hag's voice
scraping cold clouds.

The Hanged Man wakens
from an unintended snooze.
His head bobs slightly
as he sets about moping.

Oddly enough, he's
an excellent dancer
and she's not half bad.
They have this in common too:

it's all my fault; if I cared,
I'd be able to read their minds.
What else is a leader for?
Odder still, they both nominated me.

I was standing on this very beach.
The sky was preparing for sunset.
Sand lay in ripples like prehistoric skin.
I remember a tide pool with a blue heron.

I was watching the heron take steps.
I was focusing on the water,
the way it stayed smooth.

SUSAN TERRIS

Buddha Is Floating on the Ocean

A trick of light and the white Buddha
from the beach house deck
shines through the window, weightless marble
poised on an incoming wave.
Beyond him, pelicans, a scribble of fog
across Duxbury Reef, and a mottled slice of
daytime moon.

This is a place of place. As Buddha sits
on a breaker, legs angled in a lotus,
so do I. As his hands rest,
the right on his knee, the left palm up,
so will mine. Our bodies have unlearned
laws of gravity and mastered levitation.
Our heads—fixed, top-knotted—
are only half-owned by their bodies.
Our faces,
distant now, cannot be fathomed.

Here as the moon draws us between its horns,
washes us with changing tides,
everything is old yet new.
Nothing hurts. Memory is sea foam
and flotsam. We love all yet none.
We do not blink, have no tears.
Our images stencil patterns over water,
glass, wave, and sky.
Tomorrow the sun and moon will appear again
with us or without.

JACQUELINE GENS

Visitation

For Allen Ginsburg (1926-1997)

A few days later I saw you
seated at a dusty crossroad
looking toward a vista of waterways
reminiscent of a cranberry bog or saltwater marsh
I once visited, maybe the river Styx.
A geography of immensity without habitation

where you sat on an old wooden stool,
poured over books and papers, focused intently.
One air of familiarity—your Calvin Klein
Goodwill navy blazer, my favorite;
your pens poking out from the pocket.
I stood quietly to your side waiting to assist you
yet not disturb your concentration.
Finished, you handed me a sheaf of papers,
Here, these are for you—for translation.

Then, you got up and walked slowly down the left-hand road.
I followed but you turned to me and said,
This is as far as you are allowed to go, I don't have the water rights
    for your passage—
a hitch of sadness in your voice, your face mostly
impassive, Bell's palsy making one eye bigger, your face a bit cock-eyed,
but looking straight on as we finished our business together once again
in clarity and respect, our natural elegance hanging there a second
    as we stared at one another.
I watched you walk off and knew that you were finally gone
on some other journey, to some other place.

JAMES MC GRATH

On the Wall Above the Sea

I am leaving my stone in the Burren
      on the wall above the sea.
      Each day the wall is taller.

One day when it is tall enough
      and it shoulders the clouds in the night,
      I shall reach up
      to take the stars in my hands.

I shall be pulled up
      to become the light that shines
      from all the lights in my life.

I shall erupt with the lark
      to let the bees sting the final poem
      from my fingers.

LINDA BOSSON

Déjà

From a spell where I, from a spell,
why does it seem I am waking, seem,
knew the wistful bell of a buoy,
the wan white beam of a lighthouse, beam,
the sobbing swell of the waves,
the harrowed scream of a seagull, scream,
on the carousel, on the carousel,
was it a dream in the whirling, dream?

MARY ANN LARKIN

Temptation

The sea's a high roller today
muscling in on a chorus girl,
all polished gun metal
pumping hard
under a sky dyed-to-match.
The marbled poise
and now, the pitch—
seed-pearls everywhere,
and he doesn't stop
and they keep coming,
and I *am* tempted
to curl in his cool curve,
foamy with pearls,
roiled out of mind,
in love with glitter.

MARK DOTY

Long Point Light

Long Point's apparitional
this warm spring morning,
the strand a blur of sandy light,

and the square white
of the lighthouse—separated from us
by the bay's ultramarine

as if it were nowhere
we could ever go—gleams
like a tower's ghost, hazing

into the rinsed blue of March,
our last outpost in the huge
indetermination of sea.

It seems cheerful enough,
in the strengthening sunlight,
fixed point accompanying our walk

along the shore. Sometimes I think
it's the where-we-will be,
only not yet, like some visible outcropping

of the afterlife. In the dark
its deeper invitations emerge:
green witness at night's end,

flickering margin of horizon,
marker of safety and limit,
but limitless, the way it calls us,

and where it seems to want us
to come. And so I invite it
into the poem, to speak,

and the lighthouse says:
Here is the world you asked for,
gorgeous and opportune,

here is nine o'clock, harbor-wide,
and a glinting code: promise and warning.
The morning's the size of heaven.

What will you do with it?

ON LOVE
AND OTHER
MISERIES

JUNE OWENS

Searching the Sand Bar

All that summer
the sun hot with lust
grappled with me for
possession of you.
I was a fool not
to see what the
grit-wind knew:
only the water wins
when the body lies
spread like a dowsing
stick between the
layers of tide.

Back then,
in the fast-walking
days, we grew dogs
and children   gave
them names and got
back joy   they came
and went   and after
periods of grief
however long or short
gave them to the universe
of sun and sea birds.

Now   barely under the
sand   lies everything we
were   tan and goldshot
and in the shallow of
night before the last
star slips   we dream
and the gulls cry.

GREY HELD

What I Was

The water turned blue, orange, brown
as I cleaned my brushes in the art room sink.
I was bristles and handle.
I was the chess club's logic,
nicked bishop, upright knight.
I was my mother's dream, so pure
and not so pure.
I was a foreign language, être
conjugated and avoir, divided
by every tab in my looseleaf, ruled
like the strict blue lines in my diary,
the relentless declensions of my mind.
I was my father's immaculate
Buick, another addendum to his policy.
I was nervous to drive to the beach. I was
the torn ocean and the vagaries of waves.
I loved my girlfriend's shy smile, the softness
of her terrycloth, her auburn hair that kicked
free from her tortoiseshell barrette.
I wanted to be the muscling boardwalk,
the stacked surfboards, the racks of T-shirts,
the shark teeth, but I was penny candy, taffy
pulled to the limit.

ALEX GREEN

The Island Not Always at Night

When she walked to the edge of the water,
her top giggling in the sand behind her,
the old guy said something
and his wife said something else.
I stopped throwing rocks in the water,
felt my voice crack in my shoulders
and tried to stand like a contender.

So she walked like the best swimsuit model in the world,
who had changed her mind about the swimsuit, and the world,
and headed back into the sea
where things were probably simpler.
I stood and watched,
leaned back and pretended to stretch,
my neck ridiculous and sideways.

But a few things:
When the wind blew her hair, I did this with my hands.
I let sand fall down the back of my throat.
"Later the piano player from New Jersey told me
I've been to a lot of places more than once,
but when I close my eyes, I am living
in the city that is truly waiting for me."

In my room I wrote in my journal:
She did cartwheels with her clothes off.
Went out for dinner with mom and dad.
Can't sleep at night.

There isn't much else.
Of course there have been others
with equal bits of impossible,
but none have made me wish
I was grinning silly and curly again,
with outgrown trunks and a glowing waist.
But it's barely her fault—
she didn't know that even if I really could
skip a rock all the way back to San Francisco,
I wasn't old enough to steal a boat,
put the helm in my hands,
and feel the ocean in the veins of the wood.
I was too young to hold her body where I wanted,
and tell her how it used to be like drowning.

JULIE GAMBERG

Casual Sex

It begins like a track team meet
or a horse race—
the gun goes off
and we are suddenly in the thick
of things.

No, it begins like a wipe-out,
your lips and hands a confusion and crush
recall a documentary about Mavericks,
that great unruly wave that kills
or delights surfers each winter

Who wear like a badge of honor the memory
of staying under for two whole wave cycles.
They say that the memory
is of the survival and not the crush
The trick is you must not breathe
the surfers say, and *hold still.*

I tell you how to go, slower then fast, then pause
and it is like the whole of the ocean
is under my command
and I can see you now past the crash.

Post-impact, I rest my lips, my tongue
between your neck and shoulder
let my hands move down the length of you.

After, I will dress quickly, endure conversation, stilted
pauses as intimacy dissolves like a compressed pill
in a warm sea, first powder, then dust, then nothing.

JIM DEWITT

Secluded Beach

together we rose
climbing from the soaring surf
crashing
all-skin bodies unisoned
      to catch the magic
           browning sun . . .
spread eye-far
the squeaking sand a foundry
hot moulding
our face-down shapes
         together
we waned the day

CAROL HOBBS

You Said We Almost Fell in Love

There is an iceberg so big I have to drive my car
to different vantage points along the shore
to understand something of its perimeter.
It is high, a flat plateau, pristine.
If I lie in the middle of that ice island, I am
part of some new nation and the edge of it
is a long journey I might prepare for.
Or ignorant of edge, I live
all shining at the crystal center,
not seeing those others from the city
line the shore, empty shadowless people
who drive cars around the outside rim of my perfect world.
Their headlights become part of the bowl of stars.
This is a paradise. I have a perfect life.
I am untouched by edges.
I am in love without any idea of what it is
to fall.

MICHAEL FOSTER

Matrimonial

The moon rises
full out of the Atlantic
and paves a pewter highway
to the shore. Trawlers,
heavy with catch,
arms splayed upward,
crawl through the light
toward Little River Inlet.
Water closes behind them.
You are asleep, risking madness,
behind an open curtain.

This morning
you woke me at first light
your near leg thrown across
my hip. Our rhythms,
until we trembled,
celebrated heartbeat,
celebrated the old return
of water to the earth.

Always,
even the hard years
when we reopened
each other's wounds,
water closed behind us
and we healed.

CAROLINE FINKELSTEIN

Vineyard

Casa is for house and house is for the body
and body is the ocean at beautiful Lucy Vincent beach.

I stood there breathing in. At the beach that nears Menemsha,
I saw scavenging, gritty gulls, poor golden-footed gulls,

saw cliff swallows looping and returning.
And the roses looked like pillows—big and full—

the candle-colored roses were as cool and wide as basins
in the house, silken roses day and night.

At dawn I heard the towhees.
There were purple stones throughout Menemsha,

and shrubs, and many trees. I had my Field Guide,
my paradox, my wooden bridge of now and then:

I remembered when I kept a memory of my father
dying even as he breathed. *He* had his stricken soul

and I knew him for a broken house,
a sullen, reckless man. Reckless was the loneliness.

House of canary yarrow,
I was a ghost but so was everyone.

Lonely was the body, even as it looked
for love, a flimsy, tender wing on water.

I touched my husband's upper arms.
So much desire, so much willful chicory and luxury.

I tasted salt and peaches. The wind was soft. I slept.

I Was My Own Invention; My Realities Turned Pastel

as the rest of the world continued alongside famous others
as church-doors flew wide open
as the argument of Vivaldi
went into dark G minor and was a thunderstorm
as half the world puttered and the other half wept
as everything tarnished turned silver
as lizards in sage plants tried eating bees
in pure butterfly weather

I drove down to the sea

past undulant plains
where Florence murdered Siena
I could see the horsemen the armies
rag-tag resplendent
numerous gentians calendula fennel

I saw the glorious marble graves
and remembered abandon the name of my lover
his voice the grin of a fox
a fly-by-night goldfinch
a cruise ship steaming away

white ship on aquamarine
his fingers in my mouth
the blind places the islands
05715-90932
ringing and ringing—

BRITTANY T. PERHAM

Love Poem

The body has tried easing the heart
with lovers. The body has tried
by leaving them. The body is the beach
at its most undone—water has folded
back to its furthest perimeter
and is almost lost. You know this
coast: the line of seaweed, rock and mussel shell,
the softest field of sand that will hold
your weight and then release you.
Who does not want to be lost this easily?
All day, you walk the margin
for what can be taken in the hands.
When it's late enough you go
toward home, each pocket filled with stones.
You are determined to have them all, determined
that not one may be left, certain
that all their lives they've longed for you.

CAROL DINE

At Sea

If you can be with a man
on the ocean,
you can be with him anywhere,
she tells herself,
heading for open water.
He shoots the sun with his sextant.
She wants danger, the edge
where the heart quickens
and later, to be safe.

* * *

It is her watch tonight
as ten foot waves ride her
to the top, then down into the trough.
He takes the helm,
checking the trim of the sails.
She envies his eyes.

* * *

She loves him when the storm
becomes gentle, and the moon
catches in his beard.
When they kiss,
she saves his breath in her mouth.

Sometimes she thinks of him
as the enemy
in their tight cabin,
he stinking of sea salt,
she feeling the boat
pitch beneath her thighs.

* * *

On the fourth day out,
black clouds, a rogue wave
port side, and the jib sheet loose.
He yells *Dammit, cut the line*
his eyes wild,
as if she had made the storm.

* * *

Winds, rain for days.
They are steeping in brine,
their skin raw and gray.
From the cockpit,
they watch the spreader lights
fallen like stars
at the mercy of tides.

LOUIS PHILLIPS

Seascape

We never had it
So good,
Atlantic chill 1/2 block
Away, constant swell at

Our window, green
Crag of
An ocean straining
Its spine,

$174 a day
For an ocean,
But you,
Angry,

Lying like a beach
On another's bed,
Farther away
Than the moon's

Proud wake.

MICHAEL COLONNESE

The Outer Banks

Light crowns on waves unblamed,
the crescent moon and unpoured whiskey
saved for later. One marriage on the rocks.
High seas run till overthrown, spun off,
out, to hit and break like horseshoe crabs
to shell and spine. Waves come again,
again, and harder, crawl in, retreat.

Rain pelts our wooden roof. Beneath
Torn tidal nets of selflessness and stars,
Where latinate apologies are hung to dry,
stretched out and useless, your sobs
tell six cracked buoy bells the pretty
inside way of things. We've come
so far and wrecked, found shallows, shoals.

DAVID STARKEY

Still Life

My ex-wife may be anywhere now,
but I always picture her

sitting down to coffee

on the porch of a beachfront home.
On the table, draped with linen,

a pail of yellow roses,

a bowl of sliced cantaloupes,
oranges and limes. Gazing

out at evening surf, she fingers
a string of pearls. And the man

she waits for isn't me.

ALLEN C. WEST

Letting Go

You can't make love to a ghost
Leave your restless bed
and swim out across the cove
toward a light glittering somewhere
water warmer than air
the shore darker than its reflection
When a beach looms and your fingers
stroke the sandy bottom turn back
toward the light shining from the dock
the way you aim for a porch light
or keep the moon on your left
to guide you home in the dark
your face turning
into and out of the water
so you can't tell how far
you have to go

Cape Cod Dawn

When the air is still
and mist hangs on the cove
like a gauze curtain
inside a closed-up house,
yachts double,

half anchored in sea,
half moored in air,
hulls fused to a surface
along which you walk the dog
every morning, feet to feet,
coffee mug in hand.

Like you, like us,
birds pair up. Swimming
gulls are Siamese twins.
Tern, cormorant, the lithe
ponderous great
blue heron

ghost over and upside-
down until the wind
begins to breathe,
leaving Hopper
above Monet.

MARTIN I. LEVINE

November

Down at the Captain's Table
the old Portuguese fisherman is drinking
to the coming of the dead-eyed

winter. A coyote and a cold wind,
hard with hunger, move through
the lean pickings of the feeding

tide, abandoned rose hips, pale
dune grasses, rows of empty summer
cottages, and the edge of the brittle

salt marsh, as the winter buttons up
the frost-whipped beach
like a man closed shut.

I stop at the red cottage
where the coldness echoes through the eaves
where a broken mantis lies

where no one is sitting down to breakfast
where your naked feet do not run wet
through the rooms

where unsoiled sheets do not rise bittersweet
on your chocolate brown nipples
where your fragrance does not fill the room

where there are no little ceremonies
where the stars mirror the dark sea
in which you exist

MICHELE WOLF

The Great Tsunami

She recognizes its crest in the way he looks at her.
The wave is vast as the roiling mass in the Japanese
Print they had paused in front of at the museum,
Capped with ringlets of foam, all surging sinew.
That little village along the shore would be
Totally lost. There is no escaping this.
The wave is flooding his heart,
And he is sending the flood
Her way. It rushes
Over her.

Can you look at one face
For the whole of a life?

Does the moon peer down
At the tides and hunger for home?

4.30.9X

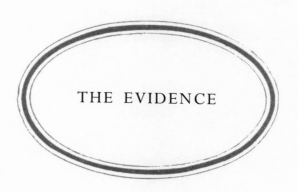

THE EVIDENCE

GREGG MOSSON

Snapshots of the Repossession
of My Father's Boat

A thin man
tips his hat,
"is this the one?"

                                        Ropes
                                        like forearms
                                        on a rail....

                My father would say,
                  "always know where the clouds are."

                                The dealer hops aboard.
My father turns to face the sky.

                                  Journal entry:
                                "I lasted, thank god.
                                      This is why I was born.

      The windless warmth
      The tap of the sea
      The toy shore
      The painted houses

                        The man says, "It's an oldie,
                        but you've kept it well,"
                        patting the smooth wood.

BARBARA CROOKER

Eating Meltaways in Harwichport

It's been four years since my father died,
and it seems like I'm becoming him,
driving my mother to this sandy spit
where we vacation with their friends
of thirty years, go to thrift shops
and lobster roll lunches at the white
Congregational church, admire the blue
hydrangeas bobbing along the picket fence.
This year, death's been busy as a surfcaster
on a moon-filled night, blues and stripers
running wild, reeling them in one after another:
Dottie talking on the phone, Merrick dozing
in his recliner, cancer's heavy weather
taking Jean and Clare, and only Mom and I remain.

We're sitting at our favorite restaurant, stirring
sugar in iced tea, hearing the little cubes tinkle
like wind chimes. I want to skip the next chapter,
stay here like this, life rolling on predictable
as morning fog, or thick milky chowder, the sun,
a pat of butter, melting through. Our waitress,
in a white apron and pink uniform, her name scrolled
on her left breast, waits with a pad of paper:
"The meltaways just came out of the oven," she says,
"Can you smell them? I can put them in a box
if you don't have room for now."

Postcards from Hawaii

The coconut palms are swaying in the Trade Winds—
Trade Winds—the very name echoes, sending up
clipper ships, cargoes of spice and silk . . .
One night, the moon was so bright you could read by it,
writing a path of silver on the restless Pacific,
shimmering, shimmering.
The next, the moon set early, the stars reigned,
ebbing and throbbing, the black silk night alive with fire.
What does this mean? What is the ocean murmuring
with its endless refrain, repeat, repeat?
Whatever is said is echoed by the palm fronds
as they clatter and rasp in the wind.
There is so much to write, in this spin of time,
but everything rattles on in its usual pace.
And these white pages with their black alphabets
have no more permanence than tracts in the sand.
Here, almost every tree is blooming:
the flame trees, the golden showers.
The air is sweet with plumaria,
and the fish are jewels:
ornate wrasse, Moorish idols, yellow tang.
Yet as I write this down, the present slips away,
receding like the coastline at Kapaa.
Surely there are people who travel, uncompelled to record the journey.
But the words flow on, sand drifting through fingers.
Each day we put on the hot blue sky like a headdress of flowers.
And at night, your skin is incandescent,
its own source of heat and light.
And none of this has an ending,
trails off like the long white tail of a tropicbird

circling over a green glade.
There is a waterfall by the left hand side of the picture.
Everything is diffused in light.

JO CARNEY

Outpost: January 8, 1989

pine barrens
wind chop
the coastline comes to winter

it is then we feed the ducks,
my daughter and I,
heading off to the creek
and that break in the ice where
the water moves

the bread in my hands
a stark handfull
against the wilderness and
the great gray sack of self
I am adrift in

beside me
my daughter moves
I realize how hungry I am
for color.

MATTHEA HARVEY

Nude on a Horsehair Sofa by the Sea

I don't know what to do with his body.
It looks smooth—& heavy too—
from the way the sofa's mahogany claws
sink into the sand. Every other wave
is brown, the ones in between a light liquor
bottle green, & the strip of wet sand
the froth laps, then leaves, is glass-
brown & shouldn't act like mud
but does. When a seagull struts by
I see the others flick their brushes
in irritation over that spot as if to
drive it away—& me, I'm avoiding
the subject, still fretting over how to paint
the word *sometimes* because the pebbles
only show when the water's had a chance
to settle. I can tell he's secretly moving
his toes along the grain of the sofa
& back, so the hairs lie smooth, then
bristle as one wave crests & another
crashes. The woman next to me sighs.
Her clouds look like dark whales floating
in the sky, her brush hovers over
them then dips down to make
an awkward dab at the spot between
the model's thighs. It is starting
to drizzle now & each wave has a pocked
& peaked landscape of its own & people
are folding their easels & shielding
their paintings with their bodies as they run

to the striped cabanas. Perhaps he will whisk
out a cloak & wade slowly into the water,
silk billowing about his fine white ankles.
Perhaps he has to help carry the sofa. I turn
and trudge after the others, picking a path
through the driftwood littered like collarbones
on the beach. I want a way to take it all
with me—the sag of the sofa beneath him &
the curve of the ocean which is what I think
the iris must look like from inside the eye.

HANNAH STEIN

Lighthouse At Point Reyes

Fog settles in
like blindness,
muffles every sound
but the pronged blast
that splinters the air
like a hurled pitchfork.
I lean against
an iron rail, watching
gulls and cormorants
fade in and out.
At the cliff's base
long sleeves of surf
erode each other
as they break on shore
Fungus and algae
paint the rocks
rust, khaki, yolk.
Jellyfish ghost
the water's surface.
The old-time keepers
trimmed wicks, filled lamps.
They tugged lanterns
up the steep risers
of a narrow spiral,
polished lenses
that scalloped
the shining cupola
like giant fish scales.
Storms battered loneliness

against the inside
of their skulls,
the foghorn and its echo
their only companion.
Something out there
on which the sound resounds
—something more than water—
throws back the double note.
Not the flat invisible
horizon, not the lowering
sky, so close
you could almost
touch it if you tried.

GWEN HART

Standing Watch

at the former site of the Cape Hatteras Lighthouse

In the ordinary light
of this ordinary morning,
the beach yields something new—
a fine crosshatching of seaweed,
carefully arranged by the night tide.
The subtle, light green
patterns mimic
meandering seagull tracks,
but these we can disassemble
and carry home in our pockets.
It's as if they were placed here
so we would find them
and begin to know,
through such minutiae of composition,
that each strand is tended,
not abandoned,
that the watch is kept.

At Run Hill State Park

You can see the water from here,
but you can't touch it.

That's the way memory
works, the glistening blue

spreads out beyond the snarled
thoughts of the present.

Often there's a boat, filled
with faces we ought to remember

the names of, people lowering
fishing hooks into the water's

bright surface, searching
for objects we've lost

or forgotten. Perhaps our parents
are out there and our grandparents

and the fishing boat is a harbor
for those who have drowned.

PAM BERNARD

Dangerous Current

It could have pulled us into the Sound,
washed us up dead on the dunes of Port Jefferson.
We were warned not to swim alone, and never
to Green Island, an acre of scrub pine
at high tide. Sometimes from the sea wall
fronting the old Waverly Hotel
we'd feel with our feet for the pipe,
laid along the ocean floor, that led out
to that island—line up on it,
the oldest and tallest of my sisters first,
and take it as far as we could, linked
hand to shoulder, the pipe descending
as it left shore, so that for a moment
we'd seem the same size. Youngest, and last,
I'd watch them as the water took in their
strong bodies to their chins and their heads
floated untethered. That day as I bobbed
backwards to shore so I never lost sight
of them, of all there was in the world,
the one farthest out yelled *I'm going to cross,*
her arms already rhythmic and sure,
her long legs scissoring just under the water.

ELLIE MAMBER

Photo, Age 7

I was this child,
standing here at the summer cottage,
facing the pale lemon sky,

climbing to my room where the bay
shines through the white curtains
that lift and fall on the sea air.

Later, tucked in, I'd hope
for the foghorn's outbreath
to ease sleep.

Here are my stones! A pail
of beach rocks next to my bed,
carefully chosen, one by one:
silky or speckled,
some with elegant striations.
Mother says I can keep three.

Seed of our bitter years,
I lean outward to the darkening
indigo bay.

AYELET AMITTAY

My Father Builds a Snail

He heaps sand into a mountain
as tall as me. His hands
press and form the thick neck,
the shell's tightening spiral.
I search the shore for offerings,
bring him two cigarette butts
for the eyes, but he says, *no.*
I want to ride her,
feel the brush of her lips
as she eats from my open palm.
He wants to take a picture, makes me
sit beside the snail, closes
my hand around the shovel.
I want to gather strands of kelp,
string a path to the sea
so the snail can find its own way.

Beach With White Shoe

Poised
on a high stretch of beach
where the tide won't pull it back
into the surf, a single white shoe
gapes open on the sand
to remind me of the sweetness contained
in ordinary things, the poignancy
of their loss.
And of beaches
where shoes flung onto the sand
were attached to the feet and legs
of men who cast themselves from ships.

My brother at nineteen. Who killed.
Who took shrapnel in the gut.
Who looked his enemy in the eye
and prayed not to be killed.
Who gave thanks when he was left
bleeding in a ditch.

Back home, he showed us
his Purple Heart. I didn't know
what it meant, could only stare
in horror that summer at the beach
when he wore those skinny trunks
and I saw the sudden cave in his belly,
the humps where thread knit
the edges of his flesh.

What if I need a single shoe
to remind me of Jim
and the question he asked:
why did Daddy let me go to war?
As if I knew,
as if anyone could have held him back.

juley harvey

icarus and neptune

marcie is afraid
of stumbling upon
itinerant body parts
on the beach,
after the alaska airlines crash
into the water,
bodies washed up
like old crabs' homes,
driftwood, legs of lobster,
unpaired socks,
bodies of sleek, soaked
seals, oiled whales, fallen pelicans,
unshelled shellfish, encrusted mermaids.
she's even hesitant
to eat fish now,
for fear
they were flying
once.

anemones in silk

i used to be
more like
a jellyfish,
without the nettles,
parachuting the rapids,
smooth, pliable, sweet-easy
flowing like anemones in silk.
now i'm more like
a bright, brittle star,
knocking on school fish doors,
hard to break,
breaking hard
on the current
of nobody's-home heart.

PRISCILLA ORR

Losing the Horizon

in memory of JFK Jr.

These weren't wax wings
soaring with the bravado of youth.
Nor was the sun a culprit,
unless its slow dip into that other
ocean can be blamed.

And the prince who was not a prince
grappled with the controls, two women
happily chattering near him. "I'm no
Lindbergh," he'd said to a friend.

                Could they detect
his hunched shoulders stiffen as he raked
over the coastline, its small lights
little comfort as he made that last turn.

Could they hear his heart pulsate
in that final plunge, or did vertigo
protect them to the point of impact.

What in us hungers to go back—
mythic wings collapsed to a young man
charting the pristine night sky.
What in us cannot reduce his yearning
to a failure to decode the resplendent instrument
panel—minute wiggle and wave of light.

TANIA ROCHELLE

Holiday, Henry's House

We're the odd-women-out, washed ashore
like horseshoe crabs, sizing up the post hurricane
construction workers, with their loose ponytails, tool belts,

smooth muscles, balanced like a meal on the steep
inclines on condo roofs. We're here for a good time,
the kind of time that lacks details, or has only details:

patterns on a bedspread, little tufts of chenille
you pick at, absent-mindedly, leaving
empty spaces you don't remember making.

Say, it's Spring Break. Only it's November,
and we're past thirty, glad for the distance, the season's
lack of competition. Last winter, at a cocktail party with John,

I was by ten years the youngest woman. It was odd,
the way other wives would cross the room,
looping their husbands away from me

like yo-yo's on their slender strings. I have my own,
I wanted to remind them. Mine walks the dog, glows
in the dark. And the whole time, he was nailing a twenty-year-old.

She wasn't even born when this borrowed house was built,
with its vestiges of our adolescence: macramé, brown shag,
the tiny pink tiles on the bathroom floor.

Family photos fill the walls: Henry and Jean, their children
and theirs, sandy toddlers watched over by two generations
whose smiles say, *safe, safe,* and *always,*

the house like God in the background. Sand is everywhere,
in the sheets, the towels, ground deep in the carpet,
twenty years of beach tracked in on bare feet,

the closest thing to truth. From the kitchen, I can see
the playroom. It's cluttered with umbrellas, innertubes,
plastic pails, things we'll push aside so we can dance.

BETSY SHOLL

Coastal Bop

At the piano's most plaintive moment a few bars
come and go,   bird quick. Was it
really blue, and did it
                            sing, that soul sting, sweet
piercing you want to repeat?

But now the pace picks up, new themes enter
and break.   To follow you have to run like
someone on a dock keeping up with the water's
dazzle
        sun-struck wavelets flashing the sides

of a boat, shadow
                        and light, little fish
impossible to catch if you haven't done it
your whole life.   And now it's quickened
                            again, full throttle ahead, open sea, water
rough and frenzied

like sharks swimming in, everything slashed,
                                jagged, fisted, splashed—done
for dashed factioned *fronned dazond*
                        addun drunned
structure cut loose. Call it
tongues not chaos, call it casting out

ballast, boat rolling barrels, boxes
                            swept and bunched at the bow,
then bump crash backlash clustered

and dumped—sounds we oh so
quickly insist into words, but
somebody's got to

                    yank them apart

for us *oost oooo*
                    keep them wild, raw, spray
aaaa in the face, dock swamped, bird
you never saw awe before
                              and ever since what
was that?

Pick a Card

I wonder if it still exists—Point Pleasant boardwalk,
Jenkin's Pavilion, old people rocking
deaf dumb and blind. Light bulbs flashing around
roulette wheels. If I blotted myself from the scene,
would the tide rush into the empty space? Or would there be
this jagged hole in the picture around which the water does its
break-and-be-healed, break-and-be-healed
routine, a photographic trick?

Couples strolling the long pier that night years ago
must have looked down and thought we were just kissing.
But that man's kiss split my lip, realigned my vision
into a tilting martini glass on the Rip Tide sign going
pink-green, pink-green, getting no place. I saw
how useless it was to try.

This morning when sleep finally settled down, folding itself
back out of me like wings, and I woke with heavy ankles,
a stiff neck, I was remembering against my will
that night summers and miles away, when I felt my arm
twist till I thought it would break, felt two fingers
force open my mouth . . .

To shake it off, I went to the community center
overlooking the harbor, was assigned the boy with the low IQ
who knows only one card trick, though he knows that well.
I settled in for a long afternoon of flash cards, Old Maid,
Go Fish. And watching that pale soft boy whose face could
not be dissuaded from shining, I imagined he materialized

from a mother walking home counting her tips, a father
in a ski mask flashing a knife. How far he must have
traveled to arrive at simple delight. He made me want
everything inside me that's been speeding on anger
to slow down and fall away, like this harbor after hours
where the cranes and dredging machines stop agitating
and water has a chance to be heard.

I can't possibly piece it all together, but I know that
for a long time after sitting with this unfinished boy
I'll be making lists of who to forgive. I'll be realizing
I don't know the first thing, after watching his mother
so tender with her fingers in his hair, hearing her tell me
there was not a better hand she was cheated out of.
The boy doesn't know much, but he can tell by her open face
that he's done something well, so he does it again.
Pick a card, any card.

CAROLYN STOLOFF

Sea-Air-Island

Block Island

Sea

flinging wrack, moss and mangled kelp
in a low hedge, you show, old wizard
where I shouldn't go. But who'll salvage
and edit your art from cool stones

on the shifting plate but me, tossed
in your junk-strewn passage up the ledge
moonstone myself, whelped in liquidity and land
polished by the grating of your breaking edge.

Air

no ninny-finned fish can know you bare
yowling on bluffs, in bayberry, only me
hunting a hidden moon with hands
that stumble on hanks of the island's pelt

risen to muff and mitten the gale
to cough fog, to match the sneezing sea.
In buffeting rush I place a sail
against my lips and blow.

Island

because you block my passage with your cliffs
holding the halved and hollow cockles
of my heart, I press my sharp shell to your flank
and soil my nails in your tough bullish back.

HOLLY IGLESIAS

Apples at Castle Hill

As though the fawn did not suffice, nor the garble of wild turkeys, to dull the opulence, flatten the foppery mocking thrift and the stringencies of salt marsh. As though our queer prints on the path were not trespass enough. We scoffed at stable and scullery, fountains brimming with time laid waste and the grand allée's tumble toward the sea. A bank of clouds extinguished the horizon, a trace of rot rode on the air. And there they lay, thousands of drops, garnet knots in rings like drunken halos on the ground.

WARREN SLESINGER

Margin

Margin (mar.gin) n-s 1. The space on a page
beyond the main body of the text. 2. A pause
in the thought process between the seen and
the sensed. 3. The edge of vegetation that extends
from the pine barrens to the tidal flats, a wetland
the eye is hesitant to enter; its nature to remain
separate from Nature, its guiding intelligence a step
beyond the physical reality of so much salt marsh:
the sun a shadowy white against the green tussocks
of cordgrass, the flight-dragging feet of the egrets,
the sagging planks of a spindly pier; sameness
in a sinuous maze of stalks and blades; the heat
seething with insects, a glittering swarm; numberless
fiddler crabs scuttling down identical holes; dull hunks
of gurgling mollusks in the gleaming muck; so much
seepage that a stream curves and cuts through the silt
to the sea, a shimmering expanse. 4. The broad surface
of an observed phenomenon from which an inference
is drawn: Science assumes a subject in fact and form,
but its origin remains half-hidden in the *margin*.

VERANDAH PORCHE

Small Point, ME

This is my husband's
mother's summer habitat:
squat pines, scorch on the rocks.
The Protestant sands we tread
at the season's end almost belong
again to lobstermen. By the time
she has us over, the water
loses its hoarded warmth.

It's a far cry from
Rockaway Beach where the immigrant
sea was the sweat of the brow,
and my grandfather, the garment cutter,
pretended he knew how to swim.

My husband's at home here.
Without my claim on her,
my daughter could be too.
He gathers picturesque debris
for an assemblage. He names
the important birds and boats
by their breeds.

A year and a half from the amnion,
our daughter stands hip-high
against the sword gray sea.
She braves the surf, naked
from toe to waist. I zip the winter
jacket's mock-fur collar

to her ears.
The next wave could roll in like
a late-model, dull silver car and that
would be the last I'd know of her.
What if my hand-hold's nothing
but a half-hitch anyone familiar
with complex knots might untie?

Even through densest mist
his people can distinguish
what they need to. Not me though.
Who's who here confuses me.
Old money speaks in tongues.
Even the sea's simultaneous
translation tries to drive home
the same small point:

Scavengers with pedigrees own
what's where they land.
All it says aloud is
Shhhhhhhh!

ALAN ALBERT

Bocce

My uncle used to play bocce on the beach.
He stood in the sun and forgot about the water,
forgot about business and being married,
and rolled the balls on the sand. Did I ever
see him in the water? I don't think so.

He wore a bathing suit and walked barefoot
but he never swam. I never saw him in the water
with my cousin who had a short marriage and a Volkswagen
and an architectural degree. You always had to pay him
back when you borrowed a nickel. Once I saw a picture

of my uncle with the two of them, Stephen,
the architect, and his sister, Margie, who was
standing at his side. My aunt wasn't in the picture.
Perhaps she had taken it. That was when my uncle
still had an interest in horse racing and the developing

of certain personal businesses we always heard about,
since he always came to my father for the dough.
My uncle kept playing bocce after the game had ended,
kept rolling the ball in his head,
kept hearing the small, solid hit.

LARRY LEFKOWITZ

At the Shore

Redolent still . . . the odor of linoleum
Which covered the kitchen floor
At our rented place at the shore.
As real as the dry ice
Which cooled the ice box.
Burning our fingers if we dared
Touch it. Best of all the smell
Of the sea, and the reel of the sand
Under barefeet, inside on the linoleum
Where the wind and we tracked in the grains,
And outside where I stood the tin soldiers
In the warm sand.

Childhood is tied to things.
Like the paper cones of french fries we ate
On the boardwalk at night
Between putting a nickel on the games of chance.
And the two women lying side by side
In their iron lungs to receive donations.
And the eternally laughing witch
Enticing children to enter the fun-house.
But most of all the bay bridge
My brother and I contested to first sight,
For it meant we had arrived
And would soon behold the sea.

Even the rainy days were special
And we walked in wet sand
To where, under the boardwalk, lay

All sorts of dirty and threatening discards
Suggesting forbidden adult things,
As forbidden as the German submarine
Rumored to lurk off shore,
As dark as the boardwalk lamp covers
Hiding telltale lights from submarines.

Other shores I have seen since
But none sensed like that
Of my childhood, which stretches gloriously and as
Inflatable at will as the bellies of tickled blowfish
And as lightly as the little sea crabs
Scuttling ahead of the wave
To bury themselves until the wave has passed.

HENRY M. SEIDEN

What Is It About Water

that we're always comparing it
to other water? Like the last tide; or how yesterday,
it seems, the waves were rougher; or what we swam in
on another coast. Or carried up in buckets
to build castles with when we were kids. To the pond
I swam in as a child and my father thought Lake George
was colder. Or the way it was, my father said, when
he was a kid and his father tossed him into the surf
at Rockaway.

Once, in the sand at Coney Island,
I found a pocket watch, inscribed *To Monseigneur F . . .*
I looked him up and brought it back to him.
He tells me he's retired now and time is on his hands
and he takes the D train from Midtown out to Coney—
which takes him back: to the Danube before the War
& diving for the coins that tourists tossed to naked boys
and that, he says, was *water*.

My own father's own
gold standard was Jones Beach. You had to drive
an hour out from the Bronx to get there—which we did
when I was ten in a '49 Nash Ambassador. The uplift!
The *difference* from the Rockaway that he remembered!

And as for Longnook Beach in Truro: Yes, he said, yes,
beautiful—how the sand cliffs slope down to the sea,
and, yes, the clarity. The two of us are floating on our backs
beyond the line of breakers. He turns and does a stroke
or two of his sweet & measured crawl. Like Jones! he calls,
from a little distance now, except the waves were bigger!

SCHAMOMCHI
Nose into to Beach at
Vineyard Haven   09/21/95

ARRIVALS,
DEPARTURES

CRISTINA T. LOPEZ

Sandy Sunny Summer Seas

I loved that beach
Like
I loved the summer.
It was inviting,
Enticing,
Exciting,
And then it dragged on
And on.
I couldn't wait for it to end.
I couldn't wait to go home
And shower
And watch *Family Ties*
And eat a hot dinner
And feel warm
And toasted
From the summer sun.
But I loved that beach for what it was.
It was escape from the boring days
On 185th Street with nothing to do.
It was freedom on the long walks away from my mom.
It was boys' names that got wiped away by a wave.
It was drinking Kool-Aid my mom made "fresh" that morning.
It was putting on a sweatshirt as the sun went down.
It was the wind creeping up from a darkening sky.
It was dragging the now-empty cooler back to the car
And cleaning every bit of sand from its bottom.
It was falling asleep in the back seat as we sat in traffic
The whole way home.
It was my lungs hurting from breathing deep.

It was the seaweed in the shower as I took off my bathing suit.
It was how good my dinner always tasted that night.
It was that we'd do it all again tomorrow.
It was that the ocean would always be there and
We'd always be there to greet it.

ART NAHILL

Rental

And something else
I could never give you:
a place by the water,
like this cottage decked
in bric-a-brac,
soaked in a southerly exposure.

Here, a week-long view of the sea
costs more than what
the migrant gardener
will have saved by September,

though this sky,
so much darker than ours,
is egalitarian, and its depth
more than another kind
of despair.

We wander outside
well past caring
about the lateness of the hour
or the way betrayals float
back to us on currents
of too much wine;

you wonder aloud how many
of these unfamiliar stars
are merely shrapnel of light
in our vulnerable eyes,
and then, what we would give
for such faint brilliance—

WENDY MNOOKIN

Summer Rental

Our first night in the cottage
we can't sleep,
though you have brought your pillow,
I remembered ginger tea.
We lie awake, staring
at moonlight flooding the length of ocean.

The children spend hours
peeling sunburnt skin from each other's backs.
I lie on the deck, astounded
by red, roses draping over the trellis,
heavy as fruit.

Sand castles grow more elaborate—
winding moats, turrets.
Come in, come in, it's time for dinner,
my voice lost in the greed of ocean air.

Over the couch, someone has draped
a shawl embroidered with peacocks.
Like a shell held to the ear,
echoing waves,
the smallest child cries.

Maybe we shouldn't have left.
Maybe we shouldn't have come.

STEPHANIE BRESNAHAN

Night Cook

He counts ten lobsters into roiling pots
and waits for their bright-red death
then serves the humid crowds.

When he steps out back to smoke,
he tastes the marsh, the breathless murky scent of silt,
the dusk.
Reds and yellows, a white cloud stretched too thin.

The boardwalk swells with invisible sounds:
panthers, a snake hissing
where blinking doesn't clear the eyes.

Later, a sliver of moon
mounts the rim of dunes.
He knows the stars in the harbor. His.
He swims his way into night,
a slow and subtle intensity of light.

BRADLEY EARLE HOGE

The Coushata Return

Maybe my reason for choosing the marsh for my field studies was the way
it always returned to the beauty I entered as I left. The way the sea of
purple Louisiana irises parted for my airboat then came back together like
labia behind me as I moved on. The way nutria and alligators slipped
piously like Venezians from the banks of bayous as our boat passed but
were always back sunning themselves whenever I returned. The way birds
I chased ascended to avoid me but always landed a few yards away, as if I
were simply an imposition, not a threat. The way oyster shells discarded
from our lunches contributed to the Indian midden islands we stopped on,
blending in as if time hadn't played a role and the Coushata could return to
claim their land. The way footprints disappeared into muck with sucking
sounds muffled only by eddies of black sulfurous water, and tall chord
grass engulfed me as I waded through it, leaving its gummy stickiness like
logger's orange paint, attracting mosquitoes and deer flies. The way mud
sank around my ankles, drawing me in to my knees, as I vibrated long
cores into the ground. Attempting to take me with it into the history I was
looking for.

ROBIN PELZMAN

Escaping the Vacation

The bay lets me in, doesn't dispute
anger. I float on my back, feel small
jellyfish undulating all around me, so many
I am suspended in their bodies. The sky
is porcelain, a plate never dropped, the blue
from a pristine paintbox. It's shallow here
so I let myself sink to the soft sand
on the bottom, face, hair and shoulders
sun-gilded, the rest of me only suggested
by shadow. That's how I'd like to see
myself, as disembodied, incapable
of washing any more dishes, of picking
playdough off the carpet, of doing much
of anything except this. For this hour,
only I know how I am joined together.
I rest in that heaven, this water.

PATRICIA CUMMING

Midsummer

for Julie, Sue, Sarah, and Beka

     rain in torrents has washed out the road
already; out-of-season, a hurricane

is predicted. The sun shines, but the wind
strengthens, the waves

reflect gray. The children
are restless, they've been shouting

all day; winter tore us to rags, it was not
well spent; now the nights will lengthen

again and the fireflies will blink
out. The children, relentless, insist

on the beach; I take them, they fling themselves
into the water before I can stop them; and the tides

shift, the waves
rise. I cry out, "Come back, come

back!" and call over and over their names,
lost in the wind; they have gone

all the way to the high rock; they climb
to the shoulder, slippery with the seaweed and spray;

they hesitate, balance, and plummet
into huge waves,

trumpeting, charging like elephants.
I count

heads and can't find two in the gray
sea. No one

is near, I can't do
anything. I wait, hating

myself forever on the dry empty beach, miles away.
Then I see them rise on the crest of a wave,

one, then the others; they all come
to shore, breathless, wild-haired, in triumph.

- - - - -

Later. The clouds have lifted, they blow
across a full moon. The children fight over supper,

their stretched voices rise, they're at war
with themselves, with each other, they want

justice—"Go out!"
I tell them, "it's Midsummer's Night!"

Now they dance, arms wide to the white, stormy moon.
I chase

them off the roof, from the edge
of the well, and out of the poison ivy;

it's the longest day of the year, the wind
has blown me to tatters, forewarns me of more

disorder, but the children sing
at the fireflies, leap on the edges

of shadows, lunatic, wild: they are breaking
the tomatoes, trampling the iris

and dahlias, they are bruising their feet
on branches, they are dancing,

dancing.

The House Where We Live This Summer

wavers, vanishes, a shimmering mirage;
the meadows turn gray, dissolve
in the pearly light—
terror.

The children, not
aware, clamor
for the beach; I take them,
carefully.

There the light
blinds me,
striking off glass.
I lie down,
glass on glass,
dissolved, crystallized.

And still,
over and over, for hours,
concentrated, intent,
my daughters practice
the ancient, murmuring ceremony
of weaving together
water and sand,
the edge of the land
and the shining
dangerous sea.

Then, sandy, tired, they pull at my hands.
It's time for supper.
My bones knit; and the world spins slowly
whole. We drive back

to this solid house framed by willows,
backed by pines, fastened tight
to the earth's vast turning:
twilight   night   dawn   light.

SANDY WEISMAN

In Slant October Light

I've come to imitate water,
to be nobody - a mote
in the swell of sand,
the long shimmered edge
of light, one frayed towel
left by summer. To be
a gull's forked signature,
its tatterdemalion shadows,
a boat swaying on the broad
bend of the world, the slow
motion of the everlasting sea.

JOAN LOGGHE

Leaving Seattle

I invite us back to the ocean, anytime,
Where we were meant to rinse in phosphorescence
At night, our skins the stuff of constellations.

We have learned to be tidal together,
Eat Pin Cove clams, breathe as the moon breathes.
The world we exhale into grows alive.

A street singer sings us, "Cupid, lend me
Your bow." And the next street singer too.
In the celadon days of Seattle we found our song.

And the Pacific fed us oysters in little tantric
Bites. We met as if by chance
After twenty-five years of close company.

SANDRA MARSHBURN

A Place to Keep

I think of it when no one is there:
the circle of fan blades fixed in a cross,
drops of water dried chalky white
on the stainless sink. Only light
can get in. At early angle,
east northeast, a shot of sun
quivers over salt water,
streaks past palmetto trunks
and cuts through silent glass.
Like a flame it sets
yellow curtains on fire,
then skims the spines of waiting books.
Every cloudless dawn
the sun pours into empty
coffee cups left on the counter
the last time I locked up and drove away.

JOSEPH O. AIMONE

The Beach House

Like conversation lingering in the room,
The purposes of day already over,
Shadows rehearse sharp shapes in moonlit gloom,
And tinkling music of clay bells that hover
Beyond the window, harmonized by chance,
Picks out a melody against the roar
Of shifting ocean in its slow cold dance
That is the memory still aching, sore
Slow healing, of the hammer blow of heaven.
Without design the great and powerful
Lost all the ends their stories might be given,
And that's the emptiness we try to fill.
We hold onto the jagged world with signs
Like shingle on the shore as it declines.

AMY HOLMAN

February 17, 1989

Maybe the moon
was not involved that night
and the ocean was the only sound,
same sound we have in us,
rushing at the earth.
I just feel lost, unmatched
by waves. Maybe the night
was bored with its dress
and welcomed that burst
of challenging light
ripping open our house
and glowing like a Lucky tip
several bridges north.
Even Atlantic City, a speckled
lava flow each midnight,
could not compete.
I don't need
a night at The Golden Inn.
I just miss the house in the dunes
shaped like a crossroads.
We were ripping open
and beginning
to run. The fire made it easy.

JUDITH H. MONTGOMERY

As Gulls Row White

Watch with me
    for one salt hour

sheltered by red earth
    and a manzanita's arms

to witness sunfall—
    the evening-out

of blueskin sky
    and shadow sea.

The horizon loosens,
    diminishes in mist

as gulls row white
    into the gray invisible.

Stay with me
    one violet hour

suspended
    in the lamp's gold cone

shielded from the fathomless
    encroaching wave,

allowed to pause—
       for this handful of breaths—

to rehearse for flight.
       Finish.
            Fade.

Imagining Their Departure

for my mother and father

They'll leave the lawn, hand clasping hand,
and walk away through sheets of light—
like light that sheers from pebbles and pier
beached at Half Moon Bay.

The sea will invite their skins with salt,
with white foam swash beneath the boards.
They'll kneel to unlace their canvas shoes,
and dangle bare feet above spindrift.

Imagine how he will take her hand,
and point to sails flirting across the horizon.
How she will shade sun-dazzled eyes,
lean close to his voice above surf.

They'll rise, bearing the shoes, and stroll
to the pier's outmost plank—his head
bending to hers as she speaks. Their eyes
glanced now ocean-blue.

And the afternoon light that tacks and reflects
from the billow of innocent shirts in the breeze,
from the float of their loosened, unraveling seams—
that light will begin to absorb them.

She will seem to blur in a shimmer of salt,
he'll mist all glitter and melt—
while bodies, transmitting light as crystal,
scintillate beyond body.

The sun will draw that luminous mesh,
a net of sea-mirrors, into the west,
where waters deepen and twilight seeps in.
Where the sea unlocks its blue vault of stars.

KRISTIN CAMITTA ZIMET

Permission

I did not give you leave to die,
though waves kept lagging farther out
on a beach too wide to walk. Upon the crush
it grew hard to find a whole shell.
You shut, beyond high tide,
but I made you wait.

Not yet, not yet. I held you tight
by the hand, as if I still shivered at six
while the Atlantic growled and leaped at us.
You knew just when to catch a lull,
to sweep past breakers, out
to the smooth deep.

Children hang from my hands;
they wind around my legs like wet kelp.
With your brash tenderness I set them loose.
I begin to walk the edge, to make friends
with the rhythm. I can whisper:
Go now. Go.

MILLICENT C. BORGES

Honest Words

This is the sickness
that people don't get
better from. The evening
that doesn't evaporate.

I watch while his hips move.
His chest, a sea of straight
pins, and, while I hold him,
the aroma of sawn wood.

Should I bury my head
in the round ocean of his
shoulder, pretending
to be asleep?

Should I taste the salt
of skin? No, I am human.
A half body resists
what a whole body
needs. Wait for it, I say.

Wait for it. I fold my hands
into Novenas. How can I
distance myself? Out-run
his caress like an old sea

terrace? He wakes.
Each question is a test,
a piece of driftwood.
A reason not to do anything.

Is he willing me away?
Or am I tracing a slow circle
of sweat on his back against
mine? Ah! I think, a quick pull

of the lungs will do.
His moan is not what I expect.
Not what I was running from.
The tricks have worked

with others before, but he
has set me aside like a
misbehaving child. No.
Thank you. Stay right here.

Through the sheets,
I notice his sleep-rhythm return,
his rise and fall. Am I waiting
for him? Or am I wanting,
ever wanting, the ghost

that was once inside me.
Outside now but rushing
back in—if only for a moment,
a crude conversation, a touch
without words.

JANE MARSTON

A Summer Place

Her flesh is worn as if by a late storm's toll.

The widow cleans, does wash, admires
the horizon's
lowering

clouds, massive bank
behind diminutive freighter
cresting the sound
and breaching
the ocean's roll.

Alert to the kettle's warning,
she stops to think of her three grown sons
and the daughter who stays inland all season long;

considers how, for fifty seasons,

she's boarded her cottage in fall
to save something
she might come back to. Even now,
plywood leans against weathered walls,

the garden patch awaits
her practiced husbandry—

a stubborn ground to which
she clings
amid cucumbers' vine and blossoming.

CLARA SILVERSTEIN

On the Last Night of Summer Vacation

We sneaked away from the cottages,
loped barefoot down Pumpkin Lane,
the asphalt still warm from the day,
tossed our clothes in the loosestrife
by water's edge, stroked away,
the future veering off,
until rain tapped our shoulders,
reminding.

MARTIN GALVIN

Heron Bay

There is a space for winter here
To grow its ice. There is a place
For a small boat with oars and sail.
There is a piece of water here
For a fish farmer and his old wife,
Turned by the wind into the wind.
We say the night heron stands and waits
For breaking water. He knows that water yields,
That fishes break. His neck is a white slake
Fishing for the water's sake and his.
He takes only his place which is as small
As he needs. He leaves the rest to you
And me, a small boat, winter and a pair
Of old crabbers leaning into the wind,
Space for oceans to turn in, things that bend.

PETER COOLEY

Psalm

Let the sea come to me when I am old
as I come to it tonight. Furying,
let the breakers climb the black rocks
winnowing their emerald. Let the spindrift
rack the shingle and the date palm
make obeisance to the swell of wind.
Now, mid-life, I go to the birds,
tracking wood ibis, loon, spoonbill,
even grateful for this small tern at my side
whose feathers catch the last light
as I can't, ivory ruffling—
later the birds will come to me
and the thunderheads, basso profundo,
the lightning, the stars which will rain down.
Let the sea come to me that night
when its last word will be the silence
the sea maintained this noon
turning its perfect face upright,
concealing nothing, featureless,
shadowless beyond recognition.

The Sea Birds

I saw two black shapes in the rain today
divide the beach between them as they stalked
among the other birds, oblivious to all of us.
I was there to feed my flock, the gulls and terns
I tell myself return daily just for me.
Mine are the wounded, the kind I understand.
One has given up a leg, another the feathers
of his right wing, another has nothing but sockets for her eyes.
They peck at my hands, draw blood. We have our hour together.
But those other birds—they were dipped in black
so no inch of them was anything but obvious:
beak, eye, wing and claw as indifferent to me,
refusing my hand, then turning to the gulf
as they will be all-consuming when they take my body
and cease to be these words as they divide me, piece by piece,
to such winds as walk the high tide in oblivion.

CHRISTOPHER BUCKLEY

Catechism of the Sea

With a premonition of light the sea sang.
                    —*Octavio Paz*

In those days, we accepted the spindrift
        from the breakers, the glitter

On the high wings of birds as the bright
        evidence of a life everlasting.

Corroboration arrived in the alliteration
        of waves, a tender star or two

Clinging to the tassel-ends of heaven,
        a cloud, light as our paper souls,

cleaned and pressed like a Sunday suit. We were
        given to the immaculate sands,

The incomparable charity of the sky,
        and in autumn, only minor

Disruptions of dust spun up at street corners,
        the glint from mica and the foil

Of gum wrappers causing us to momentarily
        close our eyes—as close as we came

To death, unrecognized there or in the storm
        troughs spiking a slate-dark sea.

Our hearts were white as our uniform shirts,
      as the wild fields of alyssum,

And I learned nothing of set theory and equations
      scrawled across the blackboards,

Was sent out to clap erasers, returning with the unequal
      properties of silence and covered

In a veil of powdered chalk, happily, for years, taken
      as I was with the wobbly grandeur

Of the blue. Now, so much lost, so much taken away
      with the absolute gravity, grind,

Spin and brine of every invisible law, phrases
      fly out the window to no one,

More darkness recited among the stars.
      Whatever I've been talking about

No longer seems to be the point—the ocean,
      can't breathe, the revisions

Of the past will never save us now. It's all
      a fog inside me, refusing to burn off,

To offer up the rote responses to the choruses
      of salt testifying to nothing,

The nonsense it all comes to like the first
      day of summer and school reports

For science torn from my binder and tossed
        onto the winds, so help me.

Now alone, I see the clouds under sail,
        embarking out there for a port

Where the air ends, where all that waits
        for us is the heavy ringing of

The sea's dumb bells. Pick any five men
        mumbling in their coats, drifting

On the cliff-side benches, an on-shore breeze
        at their unmetaphysical throats,

And see how many words of allegiance or joy
        can be squeezed out at this late date.

Make something of the one palm tree whose green
        fronds are comparatively glorious

And resist the graceless rip and under-tow—
        it's just that way with God.

DENNIS SALEH

Decrescendo

The moon-turned pages of the sea read, The Ides of White.
Calends, candles, thumbed-over and piling old white,
the year keepsake-old, the sea an anachronism,
old before it reaches the shore, grizzled, pale.
The tide stands for the calendar, the moon the letter "C."
It's in code. "Conclude." Prepare the time you put away,
don't be rushed if it's raining hours and days,
wrap the year in white, it's time-resistant.
White is a relic itself, an idea left over from bone.
Bone and white rhyme like white and time rhyme,
like Monday from moon, like month from moon.
November is after ten months, December after eleven.
Each day fainter now before it reaches us,
comes the whole distance through the year
which tangles like a moon in a tree, waning.
Tidings, idings, time never tires of passing.
The chased sky is string-frail and could blow away.
The night is antique, the year a refrain.
It's time for something to be over is the song,
the wind taps for agreement with its accustomed baton,
let the sea end here, let the land, the year.

MARGOT WIZANSKY

To Swim With Dolphins

You wanted that,
all summer in the hospital,

a pod of machines sounding you,
pumping in, sucking out,
your legs faint ripples in the sheets.

You, who loved to sail
to the eye of the wind, close-hauled,
who taunted the rip-tide,
rolling with any wave who'd have you,
reduced to this puny adventure.

I stare at the city turned cadmium orange,
and wish you'd leave like sunset,
incendiary, streaks of fire your wake,
instead.

CONTRIBUTORS

Steven Luria Ablon, MD is the author of *Tornado Weather* (Mellen Poetry Press) and *Flying Over Tasmania* (Fithian Press). A winner of the Academy of American Poets Prize, his work has appeared in numerous magazines, including *Ploughshares, California Quarterly, Northeast Journal, The Princeton Arts Review,* and *South Dakota Review.*

Joe Aimone is a naturalized Californian who has published poems here and there in various journals. He lives in Silicon Valley and teaches at Santa Clara University.

Alan Albert has been publishing his poetry in numerous journals and magazines since 1975, including *American Poetry Review, Kansas Quarterly, Mississippi Review,* and others, and has been a finalist and semifinalist in the Massachusetts Artists Grants Awards. He is currently circulating a book-length manuscript entitled *The Stars Are Never Holding On.* He is a clinical psychologist in private practice in Newton, Massachusetts.

Shelby Allen's poems have appeared in *Wild Earth, Sanctuary, Phoebe, EarthLight,* and elsewhere. She works with incarcerated poets and is training at Emerson College to do theatre in prisons.

Ayelet Amittay is a student in Providence, RI. She is a member of Barbara Helfgott Hyett's Workshop for Publishing Poets. She received an Anna Davidson Rosenberg Award in 1994.

Rebecca Baggett's work appears in numerous journals and anthologies. She has published two poetry collections, *Still Life with Children* and *Rebecca Baggett: Greatest Hits,* 1981-2000, with Pudding House Publications. She now lives with her family in Athens, GA, where she works as an academic advisor at the University of Georgia.

Grace Bauer's books include *The Women at the Well* (Portals Press), *Field Guide to the Ineffable: Poems on Marcel Duchamp* (Snail's Pace Press), *Where You've Seen Her* (Pennywhistle Press), and *The House Where I've Never Lived* (Anabiosis Press). Her work has appeared in numerous journals and anthologies and has been awarded prizes from the Academy of American

Poets, The Virginia Commission for the Arts, and the Nebraska Arts Council. She teaches at the University of Nebraska in Lincoln.

Susan Bazett is a sculptor, painter, and potter whose poems have appeared in magazines such as *Kalliope, Senior Times, Poetry Motel,* and *Explorations, University of Alaska.* She lives and works in Newton, Massachusetts with her husband and four daughters.

Pam Bernard, a poet and painter from Boston, MA, holds her BA from Harvard University and her MFA in Creative Writing from the Program for Writers at Warren Wilson College. Ms. Bernard is an adjunct instructor in the graduate writing program at Emerson College. Her most recent awards are a Massachusetts Cultural Council Fellowship in poetry, an National Endowment for the Arts fellowship in Creative Writing, and a MacDowell Fellowship. Her collection of poems, entitled *My Own Hundred Doors,* was published by Bright Hill Press.

Millicent C. Borges' work has appeared in over forty publications, including *Hubbub, Laurel Review, Wallace Stevens Journal, Tampa Review*, and *Witness.* Her awards include grants from the National Endowment for the Arts, the Barbara Deming Foundation, and the California Arts Council. She has been a writer in residence at Yaddo and at the Vermont Studio Center. Her work has been featured in several anthologies. Currently she works as a freelance technical writer and lives in Venice Beach, CA.

Linda Bosson is an editor at the wire service of the New York Times. Her poetry has appeared in *Green Mountains Review, Hawaii Pacific Review, Writer's Digest, Prairie Winds, Soundings East,* and other publications.

Stephanie Bresnahan lives near Boston, where she writes poetry and fiction and teaches English and Spanish.

Christopher Buckley's eleventh book of poetry, *Star Apocrypha,* was published by TriQuarterly Books/ Northwestern University Press, spring 2001. *Appreciations,* his selected critical essays and reviews 1975-2000, is out from Millie Graze Press. A new chapbook of poems, *Cloud Journal,* was published by Aureole Press in fall 2002. He is the recipient of NEA grants in poetry for 2001 and 1984. He teaches in the Creative Writing Department at the University of California Riverside.

Simmons B. Buntin is the founding editor of *Terrain.org: A Journal of Built & Natural Environments*. With a master's degree in urban and regional planning, he is a website producer in Tucson, Arizona. He has published work in *Southern Humanities Review, Sou'wester, Bulletin of Science, Technology and Society,* and others. He is the recipient of the Colorado Artist's Fellowship for Poetry. His first book of poetry, *Riverfall,* will be published by Ireland's Salmon Press in fall 2003.

Jo Carney was raised as an army brat and settled in East Hampton after years in theatre, where she met Allen Planz, poet-sea captain. They have one daughter. She has a BA from Drake University. She has published a chapbook of poems, *Kon Kon's Granddaughter* (Back Street Press). Her poetry has also appeared in *Kyack* and in *Out of Season,* an anthology by Amagansett Press. She has given readings at various venues and was recently awarded a grant by the Southampton College Writer's Workshop.

Mary Ann Coleman's poems have appeared in national journals including *International Quarterly, Kansas Quarterly, The Ohio Review, Pembroke,* and others. Her work has also appeared in several anthologies and in textbooks. Her books of poems are disappearances (Anhinga Press), *Recognizing the Angel* (The Press of the Night Owl), and *The Dreams of Hummingbirds* (Albert Whitman & Co.) She has won many prizes, including The Consuelo Ford Memorial Award of the Poetry Society of America, and has worked as Consulting Editor for Emory University's *Lullwater Review.*

Michael Colonnese lives and works in Fayetteville, NC where he is the managing editor of Longleaf Press. His poems, stories, and essays have appeared in many literary journals. He directs the Creative Writing Program at Methodist College.

Peter Cooley is a graduate of The University of Iowa, where he was a student in the Writer's Workshop and received his Ph.D. He is a Professor of English at Tulane University. Married and the father of three children, he has published six books of poetry, including *The Company of Strangers* (University of Missouri; reissued by Coyne & Chenoweth), and *Nightseasons, The Astonished Hours,* and *Sacred Conversations,* which are published by Carnegie Mellon Press. From 1970-2000 he was poetry editor for *North American Review*. His new volume, *A Place Made of Starlight,* will appear in 2003.

Gloria Cosgrove's feature articles have been published in a number of newspapers and magazines. She also wrote and directed a play, *This Job is Killing Me, But I Need the Health Benefits.* Her poetry has appeared in *Abundance, The Year's Best Writing* (Writer's Digest), and is forthcoming in *Pearl* and *California Quarterly.*

Barbara Crooker has published poems in a wide variety of magazines, including *The Christian Science Monitor, River City, Yankee, The Beloit Poetry Journal,* and *Poetry International.* Her work has appeared in over a dozen anthologies. She has published ten chapbooks, including *Writing Home* (Gehry Press), *In the Late Summer Garden* (H & H Press), and *Ordinary Life* (ByLine). Her awards include first prize in the ByLine chapbook competition, first place in the *New Millenium Writings* Y2K poetry contest, and fellowships from the Virginia Center for the Creative Arts.

Elizabeth Crowell is a poet and fiction writer who has taught both college and high school students. Her work has appeared in many publications, including *Doubletake* and *New Millenium Writings.*

Patricia Cumming has two poetry collections, *Afterwards* and *Letter from an Outlying Province,* from Alice James Books. She has taught at M.I.T. and most recently at Wheaton College. She is now working on a memoir told as fiction. One of her stories was recently published in *The South Carolina Review,* and poems have appeared in many publications, including *The Women's Review of Books, ACM,* and *Crone's Nest.*

Amy Dengler lives in Gloucester, MA. Her work has appeared in newspapers, journals, and anthologies. She is the recipient of a Robert Penn Warren Award from New England Writers. Her collection of poetry, *Between Leap and Landing,* was published in 1999 by Folly Cove Books.

Jim DeWitt is the author of 34 published books and has been the editor of several literary journals, including *Eschew Obfuscation Review* and *Cephalic Thunder.* He has been a language researcher, a writer-in-the-schools, and a president of the Michigan Council for Teachers of English. He won first prize in a national poetry contest of the San Francisco Bay Area Poets

Coalition. Over the last 13 years, his poems and flash fiction have appeared in 1,879 different venues ranging from journals to broadsides, including *Poet Lore, Eidos, Street Beat, Scene-Zine, Fox Cry,* and *Kyosaku.*

Carol Dine, author of *Trying to Understand the Lunar Eclipse* and *Naming the Sky,* received the 2001 Francis Locke Memorial Poetry Award from Bitter Oleander Press. With a grant from Boston's St. Botolph Club, Carol will visit Amsterdam and the Van Gogh Museum to complete her poem series based on the artist's work. Her essay, "The Layers", appears in *Mending the World: Women Reflect on 9/11* (Marjorie Agosin, ed., White Pine Press).

Mark Doty has received many honors for his poetry, including the National Books Critics Circle Award, a Whiting Writers' Award, a Guggenheim Fellowship, and a Lila Wallace-Reader's Digest Writers' Award. A National Book Award finalist and two-time recipient of a National Endowment for the Arts Fellowship, he is the only American poet to have won Britain's T.S. Eliot Prize. The author of three prose volumes—*Heaven's Coast, Firebird,* and *Still Life with Oysters and Lemon*—he teaches in the graduate program at the University of Houston. Mr. Doty lives in Houston and in Provincetown.

James Doyle's work has appeared in many magazines, including *Poetry, The Literary Review, The Midwest Quarterly,* and *The Iowa Review.* Two books of his poetry have been published. He is retired. He and his wife, the poet Shaun Doyle, love having lots of time to read, write, and enjoy seven grandchildren.

Wendy Drexler was raised in Denver, CO, and graduated from the University of Pennsylvania with a degree in art history. She lives in Belmont, MA. Wendy is an editor of language arts materials, plays and teaches the recorder and sings with a chorus. She has a 23-year-old daughter and a 17-year-old son. Her poems have appeared in *Victory Park,* the journal of the New Hampshire Institute of Art.

Caroline Finkelstein has published three books of poetry, *Windows Facing East, Germany,* and *Justice.* Her fourth book will be published soon. She has received two NEA grants, has been artist-in-residence in Vermont and Massachusetts. In 2001 she received the Mel Cohen award for the best poem in *Ploughshares*. More than one hundred of her poems have been published in journals and periodicals such as *Poetry, Gettysburg Review, Fence, The Paris Review.*

Michael Foster's poems have appeared in various journals, including *International Poetry Review* and *Oasis,* as well as in a number of anthologies. Other poems are featured in upcoming issues of *The Cortland Review, Stickman Review,* and *The Cape Rock.*

The Reverend **Anne Carroll Fowler** is an Episcopal priest and rector of St. John's Church in Jamaica Plain, MA, where she lives. Her work has appeared in *Birmingham Poetry Review, Comstock Review, Cumberland Poetry Review, The Literary Review, Kansas Quarterly, Sojourners,* and other journals, and is included in the anthologies *Unsilenced: The Spirit of Women* and *Women's Uncommon Prayers.* Her chapbook, *Five Islands,* was published by Pudding House Press.

Freddy Frankel was born and educated in South Africa and migrated to the U.S. in 1962. Retired, and a professor emeritus of psychiatry, he lives in the Boston area. He has been writing poetry for the past five years, and his work has been published in several literary journals and poetry magazines.

In the last few years, **Martin Galvin** has had poems in *Poetry, Orion, Painted Bride Quarterly, The New Republic, The Atlantic Monthly, The Christian Science Monitor,* and *Best American Poetry 1997.* Last year he had the searing experience of reading at NIH's Children's House. In January 2002, he was one of the readers for the Library of Congress' MidDay Muse Reading Series. One book, *Wild Card,* was published by Washington Writer's Publishing House.

Julie Gamberg feels fortunate to be able to pay her rent working with California Poets in the Schools and other organizations teaching writing to homeless five-year-olds, teenagers in juvenile hall, older adults, and everyone in between. Julie received her BA in the double majors of Media Arts and Peace Studies at Antioch College and is pursuing her MFA in poetry and fiction at Mills College.

Jacqueline Gens studied classics at Smith. For many years she was aassociated with the Jack Kerouac School of Disembodied Poetics at the

Naropa Institute. From 1989-1995 she worked for the late poet Allen Ginsberg in his New York office. She is currently the co-director of the New England College MFA Program in Poetry.

David Giannini has published 23 collections of his poetry, including *Antonio & Clara* (Adastra Press), *Keys* (leave books), *Others' Lines* (Cityful Press, Seattle), *Stem* (White Pine Press), and *Arizona Notes* (tel-let press). His work appears in national and international anthologies and magazines. Awards include several Massachusetts Artists Fellowship Awards, The Osa and Lee Mays Award for Poetry, and the University of Florida Prose Poetry Award. He presently works as a psychiatric social worker-case manager at The Northwest Center. He lives in Otis, MA, with his wife, Pamela.

Alex Green is a native of California and holds an MFA in Creative Writing from St. Mary's College of California. Alex's work has appeared in *The Mid-American Review, RHINO, The Berkeley Poetry Review, The Oregon Review, Faultline,* and *6,500.* Alex is a recent winner of the *Mid-American Review* Editor's Choice Award. As a music critic, Alex's reviews and interviews have appeared in *Discoveries, GQ Japan, Yahoo!*, and others. Alex currently teaches at St. Mary's College of California.

William Greenway's seventh collection, *Ascending Order*, is forthcoming from the University of Akron Press Poetry Series, which also published *I Have My Own Song for It: Modern Poems of Ohio*, which he co-edited. He won the 2001 Ohiana Poetry Award and is Professor of English at Youngstown State University.

John Grey is an Australian-born poet, playwright, and musician who has lived in the U.S. since the late 70's. He has several works in progress and was recently published in *South Carolina Review, Confluence,* and *Bogg.*

Rasma Haidri and her family live 200km above the Arctic Circle in Norway, overlooking the North Sea fjords and mountains. Her work has appeared in *Prairie Schooner, Kalliope, Nimrod, Fine Madness,* and other journals and anthologies.

Paul Hamill has published poems widely in literary journals such as *The Georgia Review, The Florida Review,* and *The Cortland Review.* He has also published a book, *The Year of the Blue Snow* (Mellen). A graduate of Boston College and Stanford, he works as an administrator at Ithaca College in upstate New York.

Gwen Hart is a poet with degrees from Wellesley College and Hollins University. Although she is currently a resident of Minnesota, she had the great fortune to spend nine months in a friend's beach house on the Outer Banks of North Carolina last winter.

juley harvey is, by day, a receptionist at Weider Publications in Woodland Hills, CA. She is keeping her night job as a prize-winning poet whose work has appeared in more than 30 publications, both slicks and literary. She lives in the Los Angeles area with her two kitties, and continues to hunt for the perfect poet, poem, and man.

Matthea Harvey's first book is *Pity the Bathtub Its Forced Embrace of the Human Form*. Her second, *Sad Little Breathing Machine*, is forthcoming from Graywolf in 2004. She is the poetry editor of *American Letters & Commentary* and lives in Brooklyn.

Grey Held lives in Newton, MA. His poems have been published in *The Antigonish Review, The Concho River Review, Puckerbrush, The MacGuffin, The Lucid Stone, Pudding Magazine, Slipstream,* and *The Spoon River Poetry Review.*

Donna Hilbert's latest full-length poetry collection is Transforming Matter (Pearl Editions). In 2001, Pudding House, as a part of its Gold series, published Donna Hilbert Greatest Hits 1989-2000. She has just completed a novel based on the characters in the last three stories of her Staple First Edition book, Women Who Make Money and the Men Who Love Them, and is serving as Vice President of Programs for PEN USA West.

Jane Hirshfield's fifth and most recent book of poetry is *Given Sugar, Given Salt* (HarperCollins, 2001), a finalist for the National Book Critics Circle Award and winner of the Bay Area Book Reviewers Award. She has received fellowships from the Guggenheim and Rockefeller Foundations, and her work appears in *The New Yorker, The Atlantic, The Nation, The New Republic,* and *Best American Poetry,* as well as many literary publications. She lives in the San Francisco Bay Area.

Carol Hobbs is a writer from Newfoundland and a graduate student currently living in MA. She has published poetry and fiction in various magazines and anthologies, including *The Comstock Review, The Antigonish Review, The MacGuffin, The Lucid Stone, The Larcom Review, TickleAce, The Muse, Sundogs, Wild on the Crest,* and *The Malahat Review.* Her fiction has been heard on C.B.C. radio. Her awards include the fiction prize in the Newfoundland and Labrador Arts and Letters Competition and the Gregory J. Power Prize for Poetry from Memorial University of Newfoundland.

Bradley Earle Hoge is an At-Home Dad for two growing boys and their baby sister. Selections of his poetry appear in the collaborative anthologies *Singularities* and *Everywhere is Someplace Else* from Plain View Press. His poetry appears in many other anthologies and small press magazines, most recently including *Red River Review, The Curbside Review, Big Muddy, the kerf, Suddenly IV, Borderlands: Texas Poetry Review,* and *Rattle.*

Amy Holman is a poet and prose writer from the Garden State and lives in Brooklyn, N.Y. Her collection of poems, *Vanishing Twin,* was published in 2002 from Mitki/Mitki Press. She has fiction published in *Shade* and forthcoming in *Night Train Magazine.* She teaches writers how to get published and directs the Publishing Seminars program at Poets & Writers, Inc.

Mikhail Horowitz is the author of *Big League Poets* (City Lights) and *The Opus of Everything in Nothing Flat* (Outloud/ Red Hill). A selection of his jazz fables and eschatological scat, *The Blues of Birth,* is available from Euphoria!, an imprint of Sundazed Records. He works as an editor in the publications office of Bard College, Annandale-on-Hudson, New York.

William Houston is seventy years old and lived close to the ocean in Santa Monica, CA, for thirty-five years. The ocean has always been a powerful presence for him, in literature, in art, and in person. He lives in Santa Fe, where he formed a poets' writing group which has been active for the past four years.

Barbara Helfgott Hyett has published four collections: *In Evidence* (University of Pittsburgh Press); *Natural Law* (Northland Press); *The*

Double Reckoning of Christopher Columbus (University of Illinois Press); and *The Tracks We Leave* (University of Illinois Press). Her poems have appeared in major magazines including *The Hudson Review, The Nation, The New Republic, Partisan Review* and in over twenty-five anthologies. She is a Visiting Scholar at Harvard's Graduate School of Education, and has taught at Boston University and Holy Cross. She directs the Workshops for Publishing Poets in Brookline, MA.

Holly Iglesias' work has appeared in journals including *Prairie Schooner, Arts & Letters, The Prose Poem, The Massachusetts Review,* and *U.S. Latino Review.* She was awarded an artist grant for poetry by the Massachusetts Cultural Council in 2000, as well as the Frank O'Hara Award from Thorngate Road Press for her chapbook, *Good Long Enough.* Another chapbook, *Hands-On Saints,* was recently released by Quale Press. She lives in Western Massachusetts, where she coordinates a middle-school peer mediation program.

Halvard Johnson has received grants from the National Endowment for the Arts, the Maryland Arts Council, and Baltimore City Arts. He has published four collections of poetry— *Transparencies and Projections, The Dance of the Red Swan, Eclipse,* and *Winter Journey*—all from New Rivers Press. His poetry and fiction have appeared in many magazines, including *Puerta del Sol, Wisconsin Review, Mudfish,* and *Poetry: New York.* He lives in New York City with his wife, fiction writer and painter Lynda Schor.

Jennifer Laura Johnson is a psychotherapist and artisan who resides in NJ with her husband, cats, and dog. She won first place in the Sarasota Poetry Theatre Press' Animals in Poetry Competition. She has led workshops for at-risk youth and people with severe mental illness. She has been a member of a local writing workshop for five years and was a featured poet in *Growing Our Own: New Women Poets.*

Ruth Moon Kempher is the author of twenty-three (mostly small) collections of verse. Owner and operator of Kings Estate Press in St. Augustine, FL, she has now retired from teaching in order to have more time for writing and travel. After many years of living at the beach, she now makes her home in the woods with two dogs.

Claire Keyes lives in Marblehead, MA and has received a grant in poetry from the Massachusetts Council of the Arts as well as a Wurlitzer Fellowship in poetry. Her poems have appeared in *Spoon River Poetry Review, Larcom Review,* and *The Sarasota Review,* among others. She is Professor Emerita at the Salem State College, where she chairs the Foreign Languages Department. Her manuscript, *Rising and Falling,* won the 1999 Foothills Poetry Chapbook Competition.

Caroline Knox's collection, *A Beaker: New and Selected Poems,* was published by Verse Press. Her previous books are *The House Party* and *To Newfoundland* (Georgia) and *Sleepers Wake* (Timken). Her work has appeared in *The American Scholar, Harvard, The Massachusetts Review, The Paris Review, Ploughshares, Poetry,* and elsewhere. She has received awards from the National Endowment for the Arts, the Yale/Mellon Visiting Faculty Program, and other organizations. Her work has been anthologized in *The Best American Poetry 1988* and *1994*. She is currently a Visiting Fellow at Harvard.

Raphael Kosek lives and writes in the Hudson Valley. She is a Vassar graduate and has published widely in literary journals since returning to poetry in her forties. Currently she has work forthcoming in *Kalliope* and *Water-Stone* and is working on a series of poems based on Georgia O'Keefe's paintings.

Kathryn Kruger received her Ph.D. in English at University of Miami. Her first collection of poems, *Solstice,* won the 2001 chapbook contest for Poetic Matrix, and was released this past December. Her poem "Fallen", which won the 2001 contest for Human Equity through Art, was nominated for a Pushcart Prize. She lives with her husband and two children in Warrenville, IL.

Jacqueline Kudler teaches classes in memoir writing and literature at the College of Marin in Kentfield, where she serves on the board of the Marin Poetry Center. She co-writes a hiking column for the Pacific Sun and published a hiking book, *Walking from Inn to Inn,* in 1986. Her poems have appeared in numerous reviews, magazines, and anthologies, most recently *Birmingham Review, Georgia Poetry Review,* and *Perihelion*. Her poetry collection, *Sacred Precinct,* will be published by Sixteen Rivers Press in 2003.

Mary Ann Larkin has taught writing and literature in a number of colleges and universities, lately at Howard University in Washington, DC. *The Coil of the Skin,* a book of poems, was published by Washington Writers Publishing House, and a chapbook, *White Clapboard,* by Carol Allen of Philadelphia. Her poems have appeared in *Poetry Ireland, New Letters, Poetry Greece,* and other magazines, and in more than twenty anthologies. She has written for *Foundation News,* National Public Radio, and The Watershed Foundation, and was formerly a consultant to non-profit organizations.

Laura Lechner is a member of Barbara Helfgott Hyett's Workshop for Publishing Poets. She teaches creative writing in an after-school program for elementary school students. Her most recent publications include *Hanging Loose* and *Crooked River Press,* and she has work forthcoming in *Ibbetson Street Press.* "Landscape" was written about Herring Cove Beach in Provincetown, MA.

Larry Lefkowitz's articles, poems, and short stories have appeared in publications in the U.S., Israel, and Europe. He was born in Trenton, NJ, in 1937, and has been a resident of Jerusalem since 1972.

Eric Leigh received his MFA in Poetry from the University of Michigan, Ann Arbor. He is a 2002 Pushcart Prize nominee and has been honored with several Hopwood Awards, a Cowden Fellowship, and a Rainmaker Award. His work has appeared in *Salt Hill, Cimarron Review, West Branch, Zone 3, Good Foot Magazine, Passages North,* and *The Princeton Review* among other venues. He currently lives and works in San Francisco.

Dee LeRoy is a former science writer currently working freelance as a pen & ink illustrator and a colored pencil artist. Her poems have been published by *Sulphur River Literary Review, Limestone, Willow Review, Peregrine,* and *The Plastic Tower.*

Martin I. Levine has been writing poems for over thirty years. He is the co-director of the Ramapough Poets, a lower Hudson Valley poetry advocacy group, and is actively involved in running workshops in the local schools and libraries. In addition, he helps run the monthly poetry program at the local Barnes and Noble. For the last twelve years he has spent time on

Cape Cod, using the experience as inspiration for many poems.

Joan Logghe has lived in New Mexico since 1973. She won a National Endowment Fellowship in poetry, a Barbara Deming Memorial/ Money for Women grant, and a Mabel Dodge Luhan Internship. Her books include *Twenty Years in Bed with the Same Man* (La Alameda), *Sofia* (La Alameda), *Blessed Resistance* (Mariposa Printing and Publishing), and *Another Desert: Jewish Poetry of New Mexico* (Sherman Asher Publishing), edited with Miriam Sagan.

Cristina Teresa Lopez is a twenty-six-year-old, up and coming author who just completed her first book, *Finding Francis*, and is currently working on her second, a book of letters to a lost friend. Her poems have appeared in on-line journals, including *Switched-on Gutenberg, Katzwinkel.com,* and *The Pedestal Magazine.* Poems and essays have also been published in many printed poetry anthologies. Her awards include Third Place in the NLAW's International Free Verse Poetry contest of 2000 and First Place in the Personal Lyrics category of the Poetry Society for Michigan.

Carol Wade Lundberg teaches creative writing at the Santa Rosa Jr. College in CA. Her poetry and short stories have appeared in *Poetry New York, Green Mountains Review, Old Crow, Snake Nation,* and numerous other journals. Her first book of poetry, *The Secret Life,* was published by Mellen Poetry Press.

Ellie Mamber has had work published in *The Comstock Review* and *Salamander* as well as other literary magazines and anthologies. A retired administrator, she is a resident of Newton, MA and has read several times in the Newton library poetry series.

Marlboro College: Peter Gould writes: "This is a group poem written by five travelers to Cuba in May of 2001. Each poet wrote three or four lines; none knew what the others were writing. The mutual prompt was the beach day just ended. Yemaya is the Santería goddess of the ocean; Oshun is the goddess of rivers, of fresh water."

Sandra Marshburn's poems have appeared in a variety of publications including *Tar River Poetry, Yankee, Now & Then,* and *The MacGuffin.* Her chapbooks include *Controlled Flight* (Alms House Press) and *Undertow* (March Street Press). She teaches writing courses at West Virginia State College and lives on the Elk River in Charleston.

Jane Marston lives in Athens, GA, where she has taught English and developmental composition at the University of Georgia. She has recently begun a second life as a retired person. In that capacity, she has published a dozen or so poems, most recently in *Borderlands* and *Bellowing Ark.*

Louis J. Masson, Ph.D., has for many years taught literature and writing at the University of Portland and has been a contributing editor to the magazine *Portland.* Washington State University published a collection of his essays, *Reflections: Essays on Place and Family.* His poems and stories have been in *Cross Currents, Grail, Left Bank, Open Spaces, Fireweed, America, The Oregonian,* and *Calapooya.*

James McGrath, an artist, poet, and teacher, is the creator of the narrative poetry for the *PBS American Indian Artist Series.* He has published work in *MAN! Magazine, Dakotah Territory, Arizona Highways, Language and Art in the Navajo Universe,* and in several anthologies. James recently created the cover design and illustrations for *down wind, down river,* by William Witherup (West End Press).

Wendy Mnookin's books of poetry are *What He Took* and *To Get Here,* published by BOA Editions, and *Guenevere Speaks,* a cycle of persona poems. Her poems have also been included in a number of anthologies. In 1999, she won a poetry fellowship from the National Endowment for the Arts.

Judith H. Montgomery lives and writes in Oregon. Her poems have appeared in *The Nebraska Review, The Comstock Review,* and *Poet Lore,* among others, and have received the National Writers Union and Red Rock poetry prizes. Her chapbook, *Passion,* written with the help of a Literary Arts fellowship, was awarded the 1999 Defined Providence Chapbook Prize and the Hazel Hall Award for Poetry. She is completing a full-length manuscript, *Flight,* with the support of a Caldera Residency.

John Morgan has published three collections of poetry as well as a number of chapbooks. His work has appeared in *The New Yorker, Poetry, American Poetry Review, The New Republic, The Paris Review,* and many other journals.

Gregg Mosson is a 28-year-old professional living in Washington, DC, who works currently as a business newsletter writer and occasional freelance reporter. He has published poems in *Oregonian, Fireweed: Poetry of Western Oregon, Benign Chaos, sniffylinings,* and *Street Roots,* and graduated with a BA in English Literature from Portland State University.

Art Nahill is a primary care doctor in Boston, MA, and a former Boston Globe Health and Science Correspondent. Most recently, his poems have appeared in *Poetry* and *Oxford Magazine.*

Priscilla Orr is author of the poetry collection, *Jugglers & Tides* (Hannacroix Creek Books), and her work has been published in literary journals which include *Southern Poetry Review, Nimrod,* and *Patterson Literary Review.* She has received fellowships from Yaddo and the New Jersey State Council on the Arts, and is a graduate of the Warren Wilson MFA Program for Writers. She started writing when she was fifteen, shortly after she moved to Montana. She is Assistant Professor of English at Sussex County Community College and lives in Montclair, NJ with her beloved dog, Buddy.

June Owens resides in Central Florida. Originally trained as a classical singer, her poems, book reviews, and non-fiction have most recently appeared in *Atlanta Review, Buckle & The Caribbean Writer, Manoa, Nimrod, Quarterly West, Snowy Egret, Spillway, Tirra Lirra,* and in numerous anthologies. Owens is the recipient of many poetry awards, among them the Prospect Press First Poetry Book Award for her 1999 collection, *Tree Line.* She is also the author of two prize winning chapbooks of poetry, *Willow Moments* (Amelia) and *The Mask of Agamemnon* (Andrew Mountain Press).

Robin Pelzman's poems have appeared in numerous publications, including *The Antigonish Review, Concrete Wolf, The Comstock Review, Flash!point, The Carriage House Review,* and *Salamander.* A member of the Workshop for Publishing Poets and The Writer's Room of Boston, she is also the founder of FireWork, an organizational consulting and renewal practice. She lives in Brookline, MA with her husband and son.

Brittany Perham lives in Somerville, MA. She is studying English at Tufts University and is a member of the Workshop for Publishing Poets.

Her most recent work has appeared in *The Larcom Review.*

Louis Phillips, a widely published poet, playwright, and short story writer, has written some 35 books for children and adults. Among his works are two collections of short stories, *A Dream of Countries where No One Dare Live* (SMU Press) and *The Bus to the Moon* (Fort Schuyler Press), and *Hot Corner,* a collection of baseball writings from Livingston University Press. Among his books of poems are *The Krazy Kat Rag* (Light Reprint Press), *The Time, the Hour, the Solitariness of the Place* (Swallow's Tale Press), and *Celebrations and Bewilderments* (Fragments Press).

Ronald Pies, MD, has published poems in *The Literary Review, The Comstock Review,* and several anthologies. He teaches at Tufts Medical School and Harvard Medical School.

Robert Pinsky teaches in the graduate creative writing program at Boston University. He is poetry editor for the online magazine *Slate,* and he reads poems as a contributor to public television's *The NewsHour with Jim Lehrer.* He is the author of six books of poetry, most recently *Jersey Rain,* five books of criticism, and numerous translations. Pinsky is co-editor of *America's Favorite Poems* and the more recent *Poems to Read,* both anthologies that grew out of his Favorite Poem Project. He served as Poet Laureate of the United States from 1997-2000.

Verandah Porche has been based in rural Vermont since 1968. She has published two books of poems, *The Body's Symmetry* and *Glancing Off,* and has created a series of community-based projects in nursing homes, hospitals, factories, literacy and crisis centers, and a 200-year-old tavern. She developed a practice, "told poetry", to enable people who need a writing partner to preserve and share personal stories. Her residencies are at Real Artways in Hartford and in Randolph, VT. In 1998, the Vermont Arts Council awarded her Citation of Merit, honoring her contribution to the cultural life of Vermont.

Marjorie Power has published four books of poetry: *The Complete Tishku, Cave Poems,* and *Tishku, After She Created Men,* all from Lone Willow Press, and *Living With It* (Wampeter Press). Approximately 250 of her poems appear in various magazines and journals, including *The Atlanta*

Review, The Cream City Review, Ekphrasis, The Malahat Review, The Seattle Review, Southern Poetry Review, Writers Forum and others. She has also published poems in ten anthologies. She holds a BA in English from San Francisco State University. She is married and has a 28-year-old son.

Tania Rochelle's poems have appeared in several print and online magazines, including *Iris, New York Quarterly, Snake Nation Review, The Drunken Boat,* and *Three Candles,* as well as in the anthologies *Split Verse* and *We Used to be Wives.* She lives with her husband and four children in Marietta, GA, and teaches creative writing at Portfolio Center in Atlanta.

Zack Rogow's fourth book of poems is *The Selfsame Planet* (Mayapple Press). His Greatest Hits: 1979-2002 is forthcoming from Pudding House Publications. His work has appeared in magazines from *American Poetry Review* to *Switched-on Gutenberg.* He translates French literature and was a co-winner of the PEN/Book-of-the-Month-Club Translation Award for *Earthlight* by Andre Breton. He won a Bay Area Book Reviewers Award for his translation of George Sand's novel, Horace. His essays and reviews have appeared in *The New York Times Book Review, AWP Writer's Chronicle,* and others.

William Pitt Root teaches at Hunter College in NYC and has recent work in *The Atlantic, Manoa, Poetry, Artful Dodge,* and other magazines. *Trace Elements from a Recurring Kingdom* is his most recent collection. He's held Guggenheim, Rockefeller, and Stegner Fellowships, and received a grant from the National Endowment for the Arts.

Lee Rudolph is a mathematician. He lives in Acoaxet, MA. His collection of poetry, *Curses,* was published by Alice James Books.

Natasha Sajé's first book of poems was *Red Under the Skin* (Pittsburgh). New poems, essays, and reviews appear in *The Gettysburg Review, The Kenyon Review, New Republic, Parnassus, Shenandoah,* and *The Writer's Chronicle,* among others. Saje teaches at Westminster College in Salt Lake City and in the Vermont College MFA in Writing Program.

Dennis Saleh's last book of poetry won the first chapbook competition from Willamette River Books: *This Is Not Surrealism.* His poetry, prose, and artwork appear widely in such magazines as *ArtLife, Montserrat Review, Prairie Schooner, Psychological Perspectives,* and *Social Anarchism.* Selections of his poems are also in two recent California anthologies.

Karen Scoon is the recipient of the Robert Frost Foundation Award for Poetry and the Ann Mayberry Poetry Award. Her work has been published by *Yankee, Conscience, The Christian Science Monitor, The Antigonish Review,* and others. Karen has taught poetry and writing at the University of New Hampshire and at Simmons College. She lives in New Hampshire with her family.

Joanna Catherine Scott was born during an air raid over London, raised in Australia, and migrated to the US in 1976. She is the author of *Indochina's Refugees: Oral Histories from Laos, Cambodia, and Vietnam,* and two novels, *Charlie and the Children* (VVA Veteran Book-of-the-Month) and *The Lucky Gourd Shop,* which was a *Book Sense* Top Ten Titles pick. Her chapbooks, *Birth Mother, Coming Down from Bataan,* and *New Jerusalem,* have all won prestigious awards. Most recently, she received the Americas Review Prize for Social Poetry and the North Carolina Poet Laureate Award.

Henry M. Seiden is a psychologist and psychoanalyst. He lives and practices (in the winter) in Forest Hills, NY, but spends as much of the summer as he can in Truro on Cape Cod. He has published poems in *Poetry* magazine and a number of other literary and professional magazines.

Betsy Sholl lives in Portland, ME, where she teaches at the University of Southern Maine and in the Vermont College MFA Program. She is a founding member of Alice James Books. Her two most recent books are *The Red Line* (Pitt Poetry Series), which won the 1991 Associated Writing Programs' award series in poetry, and *Don't Explain* (University of Wisconsin), which won the University of Wisconsin's Felix Pollack Prize. She also published a chapbook, *Coastal Bop.* Her poems have appeared in many journals and anthologies. She received an NEA Fellowship and a Maine State Writer's Grant.

Maxine Silverman's poetry has been published as a chapbook, *Survival*

Song (Sunbury Press), and in several anthologies. Most recently her work was cited honorable mention for the 2002 *Nimrod/* Pablo Neruda Award in Poetry and will appear in a forthcoming issue of *Nimrod*. A native of Sedalia, Missouri, she now lives with her husband and two sons in the Hudson River Valley.

Clara Silverstein is a writer and editor at the Boston Herald. Her poetry has been published in *Sow's Ear, Sojourner, The Larcom Review, Peregrine,* and the *Anthology of New England Writers.* She is Program Director of the summer Writer's Center at Chautauqua, NY.

Matthew S. Sisson owns and operates a steel fabricating and erecting business. He lives west of Boston with his wife and three children. His most recent publication was in *Poetry Motel.*

Warren Slesinger graduated with an MFA from the Iowa Writers Workshop. His poetry has appeared in *The American Poetry Review, The Antioch Review, The Iowa Review, The Nation, The Northwest Review,* and other literary magazines. He has received an Ingram Merril grant and has been in residence at the Yaddo and MacDowell colonies for writers. He has also been a poet-in-the-schools in several states. In 1985 he founded The Bench Press, a small press that publishes poetry, fiction, and non-fiction. He is currently teaching editing and writing at the University of South Carolina, Beaufort.

The late **Rad Smith** attended Harvard College, where he studied poetry with Elizabeth Bishop and was a nidan in uechi-ryu karate. He studied Japanese swords as art objects for more than 25 years. He attended the Harvard Business School and worked as an executive in a high-technology firm. In the last phase of his life, he returned to writing poetry. He died in 1998. Before entering the hospital, Rad sent out a final group of poems; in January,1999, they were accepted for publication by *Poetry.*

Laurence Snydal is a poet, musician, and retired teacher. His poetry has appeared in such magazines as *Columbia, Cape Rock, Lyric,* and *Gulf Stream,* and in many anthologies. He has published two non-fiction books, both guides for new fathers.

David Starkey teaches in the MFA program at Antioch University- Los Angeles. He is the author of a textbook, *Poetry Writing: Theme and Variations* (NTC), as well as several collections of poems from small presses, most recently *Fear of Everything,* winner of Palaquin Press' Spring 2000 chapbook contest, and *David Starkey's Greatest Hits* (Pudding House). Over the past thirteen years he has published more than 300 poems in literary magazines such as *American Scholar, Beloit Poetry Journal, High Plains Literary Review, Massachusetts Review, Mid-American Review,* and *Sycamore Review.*

Hannah Stein lives and writes in Davis, CA. Her books are *Earthlight,* a poetry collection, and a chapbook, *Schools of Flying Fish.* Her poems have appeared widely in literary journals, including *The Antioch Review, The Beloit Poetry Journal, Calyx, Poetry Flash,* and *The Yale Review.* Twice nominated for a Pushcart Prize, her poems have won national awards. Her poem "The Waterfall" received its premier performance in 2002, as a song for soprano and wind quintet by Lawrence Frank. Stein teaches poetry workshops at the Davis Art Center.

Carolyn Stoloff is a poet and painter. Over the past twenty years she has published her poems in such magazines as *The New Yorker, The Nation, Partisan Review, Kayak, Chelsea,* and *Caliban.* Her work has also appeared in several anthologies. She has received grants for her poetry from the National Council on the Arts, the MacDowell colony, and other foundations. She is the author of, among other collections, *Stepping Out, Dying to Survive, Swiftly Now,* and *A Spool of Blue: New and Selected Poems.* Her new book of poems, *Reaching for Honey,* will be published by Red Hen Press in 2003.

Judith Strasser's writing has appeared in many literary magazines, including *Poetry, Nimrod, The Kenyon Review,* and *Witness.* She has been awarded residencies at writing retreats in the US, Scotland, and Spain. She wrote "Island Eyes" when she was an artist-in-residence at Apostle Islands National Lakeshore. She has a chapbook, *Sand Successions: Poems of the Apostles,* published by Parallel Press.

Marc J. Straus' two collections of poetry, *Symmetry* and *One Word* (second printing), were published by TriQuarterly-Northwestern

University Press. A new group of poems in the voice of a female hospital patient, *The Bridge,* has been staged at two universities and will be the subject of a museum collaboration at Lehigh University. In addition, his recent poems appear in *The Journal of Medical Humanities, Kenyon Review, JAMA, Ploughshares,* and elsewhere. A recipient of the Robert Penn Warren Award from Yale University Medical School, he runs a medical oncology practice in White Plains, NY.

Sonya Taaffe has loved mythology since she could read and told stories since she could speak. Currently she is finishing her combined BA/ MA in Classical Studies at Brandeis University, where she also sings. Her short fiction and poetry have appeared in various magazines, including *Not One of Us, Star*Line, City Slab,* and *Mythic Delirium.*

Susan Terris is co-editor of *Runes,* a review of poetry. Her recent and forthcoming publications are *Fire is Favorable to the Dreamer* (Cedar Hill Publications), *Eye of the Holocaust* (Arctos Press), *Angels of Bataan* (Pudding House Publications), *Curved Space* (La Jolla Poets Press), and *Nell's Quilt* (Farrar, Straus & Giroux). Her work has appeared in many journals, E-Zines, and anthologies, including *The Antioch Review, Ploughshares, Southern Poetry Review, Pearl, Poetry Northwest,* and others. Her honors and awards include first prize in both the Salt Hill and Literal Latte Poetry Competitions.

Pamela Uschuk holds an MFA in Poetry and Fiction from the University of Montana. She directs the Center for Women Writers at Salem College, Winston-Salem, NC. Author of several chapbooks of poems, including the award-winning *Without Birds, Without Flowers, Without Trees,* her work has appeared in over 200 journals and anthologies worldwide, including *Poetry, Parnassus Review, Agni Review, Pequod, Parabola,* and others. She has published two collections of poems, *Finding Peaches in the Desert* (Wings Press of San Antonio) and *One-Legged Dancer.* Her awards include the Strutga International Poetry Prize and the Tucson/Pima Writing Award.

William John Watkins is a founding faculty member at Brookdale Community College in Lincroft, NJ, where he teaches literature. More than 500 of his poems have been published in such magazines as *Rhino,*

South Carolina Review, Hellas, the Formalist, and *Commonweal.* His sonnet won the 1994 Hellas Award, and his short story was a Nebula Award finalist in 1993. He was elected to "Who's Who Among America's Teachers". His educational software, "The Jaws of Poetry", won the 1998 IBM Competition for Excellence. He was also elected to the All Sports Hall of Fame for wrestling in 1997.

Suellen Wedmore is the Poet Laureate for the seaside town of Rockport, MA, and has been published in *Green Mountains Review, College English, Phoebe, Larcom Review, The Cancer Poetry Project,* and other venues. She recently won first place in the national *Writer's Digest* rhyming poem contest and first place in the *Byline Magazine* annual literary contest.

Sandy Weisman is a visual artist, a bookmaker, arts educator, and poet in the Boston area. She teaches at the Massachusetts College of Art and runs an educational visual arts program. "In Slant October Light" is her first published poem.

Allen C. West, a retired professor of chemistry, lives in Cambridge, MA. His chapbook, *The Time of Ripe Figs,* winner of the White Eagle Coffee House Press 2001 competition, was published in Fall 2002.

Paul J. Willis is a professor of English at Westmont College in Santa Barbara, CA, where he lives with his wife and two children. He is the author of a pair of novels, *No Clock in the Forest* and *The Stolen River* (Avon), and a chapbook of poems, *Poison Oak* (Mille Grazie Press). His work has appeared in *Poetry, Wilderness, Best American Poetry 1996,* and *Best Spiritual Writing 1999.*

Jeanette Winthrop's poems have appeared in *Sojourner, The Sun, Women's Review of Books,* and *Antigonish Review,* among others. One of her poems is placed in a subway station on the Orange Line in Boston, MA.

Margot Wizansky, a poet and painter, has published poems in journals such as *Poetry Motel, Antigonish Review, Kalliope, Ibbetson Street,* and *The Senior Times.* Her work is included in *Grief and the Healing Arts,* and in several anthologies. She is circulating a manuscript, *Sweetie, Sweetie,* and is the editor of the anthology, *Mercy of Tides: Poems for a Beach House.*

Sasha Wizansky, the designer of *Mercy of Tides,* is a visual artist and graphic designer living in San Francisco. She has an MFA in sculpture from the California College of the Arts. Her miniature, limited-edition book, *Your New Glass Eye,* won a 2002 AIGA 50 Books/50 Covers award. Some of her work can be seen on her website: www.squashco.com.

Michele Wolf is the author of *Conversations During Sleep* (Anhinga Press), winner of the Anhinga Prize for Poetry, and *The Keeper of Light* (*Painted Bride Quarterly* Poetry Chapbook Series). Her poems have also appeared in *Poetry, The Hudson Review, Boulevard,* and in numerous other literary journals and anthologies. She is director of communications for and an instructor at The Writer's Center in Bethesda, MD.

Vivienne Woodhead worked as a researcher in computer science for fifteen years before coming out as a poet. Her work has been published in *The Larcom Review, Blueline, Exquisite Corpse,* and *The Elysian Fields Quarterly,* among others. With her husband William she has a truck garden producing heirloom fruit, vegetables, and flowers.

John Wylam's poems have been published in *Laurel Review, Rain City Review, Slant, Mudfish, Mankato Poetry Review, Lucid Stone, Nightsun, White Pelican Review, Pacific Review,* and many others; new work appears in *Riverwind* and *Illya's Honey.* He received a 1998 AWP Intro Journals Project award. He holds an MFA in poetry from Bowling Green University and teaches there in the creative writing program. He is currently seeking a publisher for a collection of poems, *Jazz and the Subjective Truth.*

Kristin Camitta Zimet grew up at the beach, in Neponsit, NY, where Long Island is only four blocks wide. Her first book of poems, *Take in My Arms the Dark,* was published in 1999. She is associate editor for *The Sow's Ear Literary Review,* and her poems have appeared in many journals

ACKNOWLEDGEMENTS

The editor would like to thank John Powel for his creative contributions to the project, Carol Dine for lending her phrase "mercy of tides" for the title, Ayelet Amittay for editorial assistance, Sonya Taaffe for typing, Barbara Helfgott Hyett and the members of the Workshops for Publishing Poets for their ideas and encouragement, Sasha Wizansky for book design, David Wizansky, Ben Wizansky and Betsy Powel for their enthusiasm.

Rebecca Baggett: "Thalassa" appeared in *Calapooya Collage* and is reprinted here by permission of the author.

Linda Bosson: "Deja" appeared in *Sierra Nevada College Review* and is reprinted here by permission of the author.

Simmons B. Buntin: "A Gathering" is published here for the first time by permission of the author. It is scheduled to be published in *Riverfall* by Simmons B. Buntin, Ireland: Salmon Publishing, fall 2003.

Mary Ann Coleman: "Escaping the Sea" first appeared in *Recognizing The Angel* by Mary Ann Coleman, The Press of the Nightowl, 1991 and is reprinted here by permission of the author.

Peter Cooley: "Psalm" appeared in *The Memphis State Review* and in *Nightseasons* by Peter Cooley, Carnegie Mellon University Press, 1983. "The Sea Birds" appeared in *The New England Review* and in *Sacred Conversations* by Peter Cooley, Carnegie Mellon University Press, 1998. Both are reprinted here by permission of the author.

Barbara Crooker: "Eating Meltaways in Harwichport" appeared in Nimrod and "Postcards from Hawaii" appeared in Obbligato by Barbara Crooker, Linwood Publishers, 1992. Both are reprinted here by permission of the author.

Patricia Cumming:"Midsummer" appeared in *Letter From An Outlying Province* by Patricia Cumming, Alice James Books, 1976 and is reprinted here by permission of the author.

Amy Dengler: "Watering the Lavender at Sunset" first appeared in *Uniquely Gloucester*, The Curious Traveler Press, 1998, and later appeared in *Between Leap And Landing* by Amy Dengler, Folly Cove Press, 1999. "When Audrey Hepburn Returns" was published by *Currents IV,* Seacoast Writers Association of N.H., 2002. Both are reprinted here by permission of the author.

Carol Dine: "At Sea" appeared in *Trying To Understand The Lunar Eclipse* by Carol Dine, Erie Street Press, 1992 and is reprinted here by permission of the author.

Mark Doty: "Long Point Light" appeared in *Atlantis* by Mark Doty, HarperCollins Publishers, 1995 and is reprinted here by permission of the publisher.

Caroline Finkelstein: "Vineyard" appeared in *Justice* by Caroline Finkelstein, Carnegie Mellon University Press, 1999 and is reprinted here by permission of the author.

Michael Foster: "Matrimonial" appeared in Rag Mag and is reprinted here by permission of the author.

Anne C. Fowler: "Under the Bridge at Abel's Neck" appeared in *Five Islands* by Anne Carroll Fowler, Puddinghouse Publications, 2002 and is reprinted here by permission of the author.

Martin Galvin: "Heron Bay" appeared in *Commonweal* and is reprinted here by permission of the author.

Jacqueline Gens: "Visitation" appeared in *Alembic Review,* Spring, 2003, and is reprinted here by permission of the author.

David Giannini: "Gulls" first appeared in *Talisman* and is reprinted here by permission of the author.

Matthea Harvey: "Nude on a Horsehair Sofa by the Sea" appeared in *Pity The Bathtub Its Forced Embrace Of The Human Form* by Matthea Harvey, Alice James Books, 2000 and is reprinted here by permission of the author.

Donna Hilbert: "Peninsula" appeared in *Transforming Matter* by Donna

Hilbert, Pearl Editions, 2000 and is reprinted here by permission of the author.

Jane Hirshfield: "If the Rise of the Fish" appeared in *The Lives Of The Heart* by Jane Hirshfield, HarperCollins Publishers, 1997 and is reprinted here by permission of the publisher.

Bradley Earle Hoge: "The Coushata Return" appeared in free-verse form, under the title "Old and Lost Rivers, TX", in *The 2000 Houston Poetry Fest Anthology* and is reprinted here by permission of the author.

Barbara Helfgott Hyett: "The Inlet" appeared in *Natural Law* by Barbara Helfgott Hyett, Northland Press, 1989, "Vacation" in *Prairie Schooner,* 2003 and are reprinted here by permission of the author.

Halvard Johnson: "Seascape" appeared in *The Dance Of The Red Swan* by Halvard Johnson, New York: New Rivers Press, 1971 and is reprinted here by permission of the author.

Ruth Moon Kempher: "The Rivers That Feed the Sea" appeared in *The Literary Review* and is reprinted here by permission of the author.

Claire Keyes: "Beach With White Shoe" appeared in *Spoon River Poetry Review* and is reprinted here by permission of the author.

Caroline Knox: "Pantoum du chat" appeared in *Ploughshares* and in *To Newfoundland,* The University of Georgia Press, 1989. It is reprinted here by permission of the publisher.

Jacqueline Kudler: "Bahia de Ballenas" is published here for the first time by permission of the author and will appear in *Sacred Precinct* by Jacqueline Kudler, Sixteen Rivers Press, 2003.

Mary Ann Larkin: "Temptation" appeared in *Wordwrights* and is reprinted here by permission of the author.

Joan Logghe: "Leaving Seattle" appeared in *Blessed Resistance* by Joan Logghe, Mariposa Printing and Publishing, 1999 and is reprinted here by permission of the author.

Sandra Marshburn: "A Place to Keep" appeared in *Flyway* and is reprinted here by permission of the author.

Judith H. Montgomery: "Imagining Their Departure" appeared in *Passion*, Defined Providence Press, 1999 and is reprinted here by permission of the author.

June Owens: "Searching the Sandbar" appeared in *Ruby* and in *Tree Line* by June Owens, Prospect Press, 1999. It is reprinted here by permission of the author.

Robert Pinsky, "The Want Bone" was first published in *The Figured Wheel*, Farrar, Strauss, Giroux, 1996, by Robert Pinsky,

Verandah Porche: "Small Point, ME" appeared in *Glancing Off* and is reprinted here by permission of the author.

JP Powel is an artist and owner of Salt Marsh Pottery and Salt Marsh Pottery Press. He graduated from Harvard University and attended Rhode Island School of Design. The Southeastern Massachusetts coast is the subject of his drawings, paintings and photographs. His work has appeared in *Yankee Magazine* and has been exhibited at Gallery X and the Wamsutta Club in New Bedford, Mass.

Tania Rochelle: "Holiday, Henry's House" appeared, in an earlier version, in *Way South* online magazine and is reprinted here by permission of the author.

William Pitt Root: "Ways Water Has" appeared in *Trace Elements Of A Recurring Kingdom* and is reprinted here by permission of the author.

Lee Rudolph: "The Return" appeared in *Curses* by Lee Rudolph, Alice James Books, 1974 and is reprinted here by permission of the author.

Natasha Sajé: "Channel" appeared in *The New Republic* and in *Bend* by the author, Tupelo Press, 2003, and is reprinted here with her permission.

Dennis Saleh: "Decrescendo" is reprinted here by permission of the author, copyright © Dennis Saleh, 2002.

Betsy Sholl: "Coastal Bop" appeared in *Brilliant Corners* and in *Coastal Bop* by Betsy Sholl, Oyster River Press, 2001. "Pick a Card" appeared in

The Red Line by Betsy Sholl, University of Pittsburg Press, 1992. Both are reprinted here by permission of the author.

Matthew S. Sisson: "Please, Call Me Moby" first appeared in *The Larcom Review* and is reprinted here by permission of the author.

Warren Slesinger: "Margin" appeared in *ISLE,* the journal of the Association for the Study of Literature and the Environment (ASLE), and is reprinted here by permission of the author.

Rad Smith: "Requiem Shark" appeared in *Poetry* and is reprinted here by permission of the author's estate.

David Starkey: "Still Life" appeared in *The Pedestal Magazine* and is reprinted here by permission of the author.

Hannah Stein: "Lighthouse at Point Reyes" first appeared in Prairie Schooner, was re-published in *Earthlight* by the author, La Questa Press, 2000, and is reprinted here with her permission.

Carolyn Stoloff: "Sea-Air-Island" appeared in *Stepping Out* by Carolyn Stoloff, Unicorn Press and is reprinted here by permission of the author.

Judith Strasser: "Island Eyes" appeared in *Wisconsin Poets Calendar* and in *Sand Island Succession: Poems of the Apostles* by Judith Strasser, Parallel Press, 2002. It is reprinted here by permission of the author.

Susan Terris: "Buddha is Floating on the Ocean" appeared in *Tiger's Eye* and is reprinted here by permission of the author.

Pamela Uschuk: "Counting Humpback Whales Off Cape Cod" appeared in *Without Birds, Without Flowers, Without Trees* by Pamela Uschuk, Flume Press, 1991 and is reprinted here by permission of the author.

Suellen Wedmore: "Gulls in June" appeared in *Nantucket: A Collection,* White Fish Press, 1991 and is reprinted here by permission of the author.
Allen C. West: "Letting Go" appeared in *The Comstock Review* and is reprinted here by permission of the author.

Paul J. Willis: "Refugio" appeared in *Raintown Review* and is reprinted here by permission of the author.

Margot Wizansky, "To Swim With Dolphins" was first published in the Chester H. Jones Competition collection, 1999, and is reprinted here by permission of the author.

Michele Wolf, "The Great Tsunami" appeared in *Poetry* and is reprinted here by permission of the author.

John Wylam: "December 31, 3 a.m., Daytona Beach" appeared in *The Pacific Review* and is reprinted here by permission of the author.

Kristin Camitta Zimet: "Permission" appeared in *Take In My Arms The Dark,* 1999 and is reprinted here by permission of the author.

AUTHOR INDEX

Book design by Sasha Wizansky
All text and titles set in Perpetua
Printed and bound in the US by Thomson-Shore